365 Days of Fear Not...

Pastor David has written a powerful prayer book that demonstrates spiritual authority. The passion, power, frankness and fervor needed, have been captured in writing. The reader will never be the same.

It is not enough to know about God's Kingdom; we are called to possess it. Being born of the Spirit unfolds new realms of possibilities, challenges and obstacles. Pastor David explains in a clear, conscious and practical way how to take authority over all resistance. Armed with this information, you will be in a position to fulfill your scriptural duty.

—Kenneth Lyles
Pastor, Lazarus Ministries
Cleveland, Ohio, USA

This is truly the most comprehensive documentation of scriptures demonstrating the power of the Word of God to nullify the destructive and corrosive effects of fear on our lives. This book is a 'must read' for anyone struggling with issues of fear, failing courage, and lack of confidence. It will help us to take our true positions as victors through the Word of God.

The books takes us systematically through the Old and New Testaments and illustrates every situation in which God's Word has been activated against the evil forces of fear. It touches on fear in every aspect of our lives. It provides us with the principles behind the scripture and shows how the Word could be applied to free us from the stranglehold of fear in those situations.

—Dr. Gloria Fiati
Christian Counselor and Psychologist
Toronto, Ontario, CANADA

A splendid and positive handling of the topic of fear. Someone has said that what we must fear is fear. Why? Fear negates the promises of God and puts us in doubt of God's presence. When this happens, we are in opposition to God and cannot expect anything from Him! Pastor Komolafe does not only present Biblical perspective but provides the reader with what to do with the inspiration provided by Scriptures as he guides the reader in what to pray for when confronted with any type of fear.

—Rev. (**Dr.**) **George Moses**
Professor, Le Tourneau University
Division of Graduate Studies
Houston, Texas, USA

365 Days of Fear Not

365 DAYS OF
fear not! fear not!! fear not!!!
FEAR NOT

DAVID KOMOLAFE

REDEMPTION PRESS

© 2008 by David Komolafe. All rights reserved.

Published by Redemption Press, PO Box 427, Enumclaw, WA 98022

No part of this publication may be reproduced, stored in a retrieval system, or transmitted in any way by any means—electronic, mechanical, photocopy, recording, or otherwise—without the prior permission of the copyright holder, except as provided by USA copyright law.

All Scripture quotations unless otherwise indicated are taken from the *King James Version* of the Bible.

Scripture quotations marked NLT are taken from the *Holy Bible, New Living Translation*, copyright © 1996. Used by permission of Tyndale House Publishers, Inc., Wheaton, IL 60189 USA. All rights reserved.

Scripture quotations marked AMPLIFIED BIBLE are taken from *The Amplified Bible, Old Testament,* copyright © 1965, 1987, by the Zondervan Corporation, or from The Amplified Bible, New Testament, copyright © 1954, 1958, 1987, by The Lockman Foundation. Used by permission.

ISBN 13: 978-1-63232-006-3
ePub: 978-1-63232-007-0
Kindle: 978-1-63232-008-7
Library of Congress Catalog Card Number: 2008900120

This book is specially dedicated to every member of Above All Christian Gathering.

He who comes from above is above all; ... He who comes from heaven is above all.
—John 3:31

Contents

Acknowledgment xi

How to Use This Book xiii

Introduction xv

Fear Not (KJV)
  Days 1-103 1-103

Do Not Be Afraid (NKJV)
  Days 104-163 107-166

Be Not Terrified (NKJV)
Be Not Anxious (NKJV)
Dread Not (KJV)
Courage (KJV)
  Days 164-184 169-190

Faith & Love (NKJV)
  Days 185-349 193-357

Victory Over Fear of Death (NKJV)
  Days 350-358 361-369

Victory Over Fear Of Sickness And Disease (NKJV)
  Days 359-365 373-379

Acknowledgment

I THANK GOD ALMIGHTY for His power and love, through my Lord and Savior, Jesus Christ, who gave me victory over timidity, cowardice, and fear.

Thank God for my godly parents (father and mother), who taught me to reverence God's Word and encouraged me in growing in the fear of God Almighty. I am grateful to God for blessing me with a loving wife, Mercy, and blessed children, Esther, Grace, and Shalom, through whom we have received grace to conquer our fears.

I am exceedingly glad for every member of Above All Christian Gathering, with whom together we confronted and overcame the fear of men.

How to Use This Book

VICTORY OVER FEAR is an ongoing, daily encounter. Fear may make you feel incapable, weak, unworthy, powerless, and defenseless, but your desire is not just for mere survival in the heat of the battle against fear, but rather for persistent victory. Hence, the need for daily declaration of victory through the Word of God establishes and confirms you as more than a conqueror.

Victory Nuggets:

1. I strongly encourage you to boldly declare the written Word of God, learn the principle, and pray the prayers.
2. You can start on your victory journey of "fear not" at any time of the year. Do not wait till the beginning of each year.
3. Your day one begins the very day you start and follow through to the end.
4. Each day's declaration may not be a one-time reading, but as many times as possible or as time permits.
5. Watch for your victory progress against fear.
6. Remember that the Word of God you confess "is alive and full of power—making it active, operative, energizing, and effective, it is sharper than any two-edged sword, penetrating to the dividing line of the breath of life (soul) and the (immortal) Spirit, and

of joints and marrow (that is, of the deepest parts of our natures), exposing and sifting and analyzing and judging the very thoughts and purposes of the heart" (Heb. 4:12 AMPLIFIED BIBLE).

Therefore, believe God for victories as you trust and cling to God's never- failing Word.

Introduction

"WE HAVE HEARD reports about the enemy, and we are weak with fright. Fear and pain have gripped us, like that of a woman about to give birth. Don't go out to the fields! Don't travel the roads! The enemy is everywhere, and they are ready to kill. We are terrorized at every turn!" (Jer. 6:24-25 NLT)

These verses of the Holy Scripture seem to be the heart cry of so many people today. Events around the nations of the world and danger everywhere have paralyzed us with fear. Terror has a death grip on our throats.

My long years of counseling, prayers, and deliverance, make me see how so many people are troubled by fear. Some may admit that they are terrified and dreadful, while others feel courageous enough to confront life issues. But courage is not the absence of fear. Fear is a snare—it's distracting and destructive. It could lure you away from your real purpose.

Ask yourself, do I experience sudden fear and panic? Do I go about life feeling insecure or uncertain? Do I feel an oppressive presence around me? It is also important to know that fear can manifest itself in diverse ways, but whichever way, be assured that you can always overcome and prevail over your fears.

Many people are fearful of death, sicknesses, diseases, evil, wickedness, and danger. Some even dread the future. Imaginative fear and fear of the unknown are twin killers of our time. Fear of man can also be a snare, not just a weakness or a character fault. This can cause you to dwell on things that are not true and live in perpetual ignorance.

In your struggle with fear, rest assured that God's eternal Word is the only antidote to overcome your fears.

Fear Not

"Fear has caused proud men to beg; strong men to cry; loving men to hate; and peaceful men to be filled with fury. Like a slave master, fear is controlling."
    —Wayne & Joshua Mack (The Fear Factor)

Day 1

It is written: "After these things the word of the LORD came unto Abram in a vision, saying, Fear not, Abram: I am thy shield, and thy exceeding great reward" (Gen. 15:1).

Principle: Protection from fear brings great reward.

Prayer:
1. Lord God, shield me with Your presence against spirit of fear, in Jesus' name.
2. My blessings that are hindered by the spirit of fear, manifest now, in Jesus' name.

Day 2

It is written: "And God heard the voice of the lad; and the angel of God called to Hagar out of heaven, and said unto her, What aileth thee, Hagar? fear not; for God hath heard the voice of the lad where he is" (Gen. 21:17).

Principle: The cry of the rejected does not go unnoticed by God.

Prayer:
1. Thanks be to God for hearing my cry, in Jesus' name.
2. In the name of Jesus, I break free and break loose from abandonment and step toward fulfillment of my destiny.

Day 3

It is written: "And the LORD appeared unto him the same night, and said, I am the God of Abraham thy father: fear not, for I am with thee, and will bless thee, and multiply thy seed for my servant Abraham's sake" (Gen. 26:24).

Principle: God's presence dispels fear and multiplies blessings.

Prayer: 1. For Your name's sake, O God, bless me indeed, in Jesus' name.

2. O Lord God, multiply Your blessings in my life, in Jesus' name.

Day 4

It is written: "And it came to pass, when she was in hard labor, that the midwife said unto her, Fear not; thou shalt have this son also" (Gen. 35:17).

Principle: Enduring severe pain weakens the grip of fear.

Prayer:
1. Through the blood of Jesus, I subdue pains and hardship, in Jesus' name.
2. In the name of Jesus, I break free from fear of possessing my blessings.

Day 5

It is written: "And he said, Peace be to you, fear not: your God, and the God of your father, hath given you treasure in your sacks: I had your money. And he brought Simeon out unto them" (Gen. 43:23).

Principle: Peace prevails over fear when God is on your side.

Prayer:
1. In the name of Jesus, I decree peace to prevail over fear in my life.
2. My divinely ordained treasures, manifest now, in Jesus' name.

DAY 6

It is written: "And he said, I am God, the God of thy father: fear not to go down into Egypt; for I will there make of thee a great nation" (Gen. 46:3).

Principle: Fear demotes, but faith in God exalts.

Prayer:
1. In the name of Jesus, I triumph over demotion.
2. Thanks be to God for perfecting His greatness in my life, in Jesus' name.

Day 7

It is written: "And Joseph said unto them, Fear not: for am I in the place of God?" (Gen. 50:19).

Principle: Never place man in place of God, for the fear of man is a snare.

Prayer:
1. I repent for ever putting man in place of God, O Lord God. Forgive me, in Jesus' name.
2. O Lord God, take back Your rightful place in my life, in Jesus' name.

DAY 8

It is written: "Now therefore fear ye not: I will nourish you, and your little ones. And he comforted them, and spake kindly unto them" (Gen. 50:21).

Principle: A reassuring word restores confidence and dispels fear.

Prayer:
1. Thanks be to God for His comforting presence all over me, in Jesus' name.
2. Thank You for Your supernatural provision for all my needs, in Jesus' name.

Day 9

It is written: "And Moses said unto the people, Fear ye not, stand still, and see the salvation of the LORD, which he will show to you today: for the Egyptians whom ye have seen today, ye shall see them again no more for ever" (Ex. 14:13).

Principle: Though surrounded by trouble, stand firm and watch out for victory.

Prayer:
1. Thanks be to God for rescuing me from the pursuit of fear, in Jesus' name.
2. The fear I see today, I will see no more, forever, in Jesus' name.

Day 10

It is written: "And Moses said unto the people, Fear not: for God is come to prove you, and that his fear may be before your faces, that ye sin not" (Ex. 20:20).

Principle: The fear of the Lord keeps you from sinning.

Prayer:
1. I receive grace to retain godly fear in my heart, in Jesus' name.
2. I command ungodly fear to depart from my life, in Jesus' name.

Day 11

It is written: "Only rebel not ye against the LORD, neither fear ye the people of the land; for they are bread for us: their defense is departed from them, and the LORD is with us: fear them not" (Num. 14:9).

Principle: Fear removes your protection and makes you prey.

Prayer: 1. O Lord God, fortify my defenses with Your presence, in Jesus' name.

2. In the name of Jesus, I refuse to be prey.

Day 12

It is written: "And the LORD said unto Moses, Fear him not: for I have delivered him into thy hand, and all his people, and his land; and thou shalt do to him as thou didst unto Sihon king of the Amorites, which dwelt at Heshbon" (Num. 21:34).

Principle: Repeated victories over fear establish your path.

Prayer:
1. I claim perpetual victory over fear, in Jesus' name.
2. There shall be no re-enforcement of fear in my life, in Jesus' name.

DAY 13

It is written: "Behold, the LORD thy God hath set the land before thee: go up and possess it, as the LORD God of thy fathers hath said unto thee; fear not, neither be discouraged (Deut. 1:21).

Principle: Fear hinders you from possessing your inheritance.

Prayer:
1. Cloud of fear preventing me from seeing my divine inheritance, be lifted up and scatter, in Jesus' name.
2. Henceforth, I step into my inheritance, in Jesus' name.

DAY 14

It is written: "And the LORD said unto me, Fear him not: for I will deliver him, and all his people, and his land, into thy hand; and thou shalt do unto him as thou didst unto Sihon king of the Amorites, which dwelt at Heshbon" (Deut. 3:2).

Principle: Fear comes with many faces, but victory over one aspect can bring victory over the others.

Prayer:
1. Thanks be to God for giving me continued victory over fear, in Jesus' name.
2. Thanks be to God for enlarging my coast of victory, in Jesus' name.

Day 15

It is written: "Ye shall not fear them: for the LORD your God he shall fight for you" (Deut. 3:22).

Principle: Fear ceases when God takes control.

Prayer:
1. I hand over the battles of my life to God Almighty, to fight for me and give me victory, in Jesus' name.
2. Thanks be to God for fighting my battles, in Jesus' name.

DAY 16

It is written: "Hear, O Israel, ye approach this day unto battle against your enemies: let not your hearts faint, fear not, and do not tremble, neither be ye terrified because of them" (Deut. 20:3).

Principle: A fainting heart is a fearful heart.

Prayer:
1. I prevail over every panic attack, in Jesus' name.
2. O Lord God, strengthen my fainting heart, in Jesus' name.

Day 17

It is written: "Be strong and of a good courage, fear not, nor be afraid of them: for the LORD thy God, he it is that doth go with thee; he will not fail thee, nor forsake thee" (Deut. 31:6).

Principle: Repeated failure stirs up the fear of being forsaken.

Prayer:
1. I give thanks to God because He will never fail me nor forsake me, in Jesus' name.
2. God's presence is upon me; therefore, I am strong and courageous, in Jesus' name.

DAY 18

It is written: "And the LORD, he it is that doth go before thee; he will be with thee, he will not fail thee, neither forsake thee: fear not, neither be dismayed" (Deut. 31:8).

Principle: Breaking free from the cycle of failure, rejection, fear, and discouragement, gives assurance of success.

Prayer:
1. I command the cycle of failure, rejection, fear, and dismay in my life to break asunder, in Jesus' name.
2. O Lord God, let Your presence overwhelm my life to dispel all my fear, in Jesus' name.

Day 19

It is written: "And the LORD said unto Joshua, Fear not, neither be thou dismayed: take all the people of war with thee, and arise, go up to Ai: see, I have given into thy hand the king of Ai, and his people, and his city, and his land" (Josh. 8:1).

Principle: Arising out of your discouragement breaks the hold of fear.

Prayer:
1. I claim back all that I've lost to fear, in Jesus' name.
2. I refuse to allow fear to hold me in bondage, in Jesus' name.

Day 20

It is written: "And the LORD said unto Joshua, Fear them not: for I have delivered them into thine hand; there shall not a man of them stand before thee" (Josh. 10:8).

Principle: Courage in the midst of fear makes you stand tall among your equals.

Prayer:
1. Through the blood of Jesus, I gain victory over adversaries and adversities, in Jesus' name.
2. I receive grace to stand tall among my equals, in Jesus' name.

Day 21

It is written: "And it came to pass, when they brought out those kings unto Joshua, that Joshua called for all the men of Israel, and said unto the captains of the men of war which went with him, 'Come near, put your feet upon the necks of these kings. And they came near, and put their feet upon the necks of them.' And Joshua said unto them, 'Fear not, nor be dismayed, be strong and of good courage: for thus shall the LORD do to all your enemies against whom ye fight'" (Josh. 10:24-25).

Principle: However strong your fear is, you can put it under your feet.

Prayer: 1. I tread down the stronghold of fear, in Jesus' name.

2. I proclaim a victory cry over my fears, in Jesus' name.

Day 22

It is written: "And Ja'el went out to meet Sis'era, and said unto him, 'Turn in, my lord, turn in to me; fear not.' And when he had turned in unto her into the tent, she covered him with a mantle" (Judg. 4:18).

Principle: Confront your fears, push them under, and watch out for victory.

Prayer:
1. I break asunder the grip of fear over my life, in Jesus' name.
2. I refuse to allow fear to overwhelm me, in Jesus' name.

DAY 23

It is written: "And I said unto you, I am the LORD your God; fear not the gods of the Amorites, in whose land ye dwell: but ye have not obeyed my voice" (Judg. 6:10).

Principle: Fear of the Lord gives assurance of victory over other gods.

Prayer:
1. I command every ungodly authority over my life to perish, in Jesus' name.
2. I enthrone the lordship of my Lord Jesus over every area of my life, in Jesus' name.

DAY 24

It is written: "And the LORD said unto him, 'Peace be unto thee; fear not: thou shalt not die'" (Judg. 6:23).

Principle: Fear of death is a destructive snare—break it.

Prayer:
1. I decree the fear of death will flee from my life, in Jesus' name.
2. Peace of God, overwhelm me, in Jesus' name.

Day 25

It is written: "And now, my daughter, fear not; I will do to thee all that thou requirest: for all the city of my people doth know that thou art a virtuous woman" (Ruth 3:11).

Principle: Confronting your fears makes you a person of excellence.

Prayer: 1. Stronghold of fear resisting my blessings, I command you to crumble, in Jesus' name.

2. My divine identity altered by fear, manifest now, in Jesus' name.

Day 26

It is written: "And about the time of her death the women that stood by her said unto her, 'Fear not; for thou hast borne a son.' But she answered not, neither did she regard it" (1 Sam. 4:20).

Principle: Fear makes you disregard precious opportunities and blessings.

Prayer:
1. I decree to my life, "fear not," in Jesus' name.
2. I possess and inherit blessings lost through fear, in Jesus' name.

Day 27

It is written: "And Samuel said unto the people, Fear not: ye have done all this wickedness: yet turn not aside from following the LORD, but serve the LORD with all your heart" (1 Sam. 12:20).

Principle: Fear holds you back from correcting wrongs.

Prayer:
1. Blood of Jesus, blot out the consequences of fear from my life, in Jesus' name.
2. I receive grace to overcome all wrongs, in Jesus' name.

Day 28

It is written: "Abide thou with me, fear not: for he that seeketh my life seeketh thy life: but with me thou shalt be in safeguard" (1 Sam. 22:23).

Principle: Fear is a common enemy—fight it until you win.

Prayer:
1. Through the covering of the blood of Jesus, I overcome the attack of fear in my life, in Jesus' name.
2. I quench the fiery darts of fear, in Jesus' name.

Day 29

It is written: "And he said unto him, 'Fear not: for the hand of Saul my father shall not find thee; and thou shalt be king over Israel, and I shall be next unto thee; and that also Saul my father knoweth'" (1 Sam. 23:17).

Principle: Between you and the throne is a stronghold of fear—clear it off.

Prayer:
1. I cast down the throne of fear in my life, in Jesus' name.
2. I reign over fear, in Jesus' name.

DAY 30

It is written: "And David said unto him, 'Fear not: for I will surely show thee kindness for Jonathan thy father's sake, and will restore thee all the land of Saul thy father; and thou shalt eat bread at my table continually'" (2 Sam. 9:7).

Principle: Overcoming fear restores the blessings that once belonged to you.

Prayer:
1. For Your name's sake, O God, show me Your kindness, in Jesus' name.
2. I receive regular supply for all my needs, in Jesus' name.

DAY 31

It is written: "And Eli'jah said unto her, 'Fear not; go and do as thou hast said: but make me thereof a little cake first, and bring it unto me, and after make for thee and for thy son'" (1 Kings 17:13).

Principle: Fear is exhausting, but faith in God makes your very last bit of strength enough for the future.

Prayer:
1. I yield my all to God Almighty, to multiply His greatness in my life, in Jesus' name.
2. O Lord God, pour out Your rain of blessing upon me, in Jesus' name.

DAY 32

It is written: "And he answered, 'Fear not: for they that be with us are more than they that be with them'" (2 Kings 6:16).

Principle: Fear brings loneliness and abandonment, but faith in God brings His comforting presence.

Prayer:
1. I'm confident of divine comforting presence over my life; therefore, my life is secured, in Jesus' name.
2. Thank God for His assuring presence in my life, in Jesus' name.

Day 33

It is written: "And so it was at the beginning of their dwelling there, that they feared not the LORD: therefore the LORD sent lions among them, which slew some of them" (2 Kings 17:25).

Principle: If you ever fear, fear the Lord God Almighty.

Prayer:
1. I repent of my disobedience, O Lord God. Forgive me, in Jesus' name.
2. Awesome presence of God, overwhelm me now, in Jesus' name.

Day 34

It is written: "With whom the LORD had made a covenant, and charged them, saying, 'Ye shall not fear other gods, nor bow yourselves to them, nor serve them, nor sacrifice to them'" (2 Kings 17:35).

Principle: Fear always demands worship—never yield to it.

Prayer: 1. I withdraw my submission to fear, in Jesus' name.

2. No longer shall fear enslave my life, in Jesus' name.

DAY 35

It is written: "And the statutes, and the ordinances, and the law, and the commandment, which he wrote for you, ye shall observe to do for evermore; and ye shall not fear other gods" (2 Kings 17:37).

Principle: What you fear rules and controls you; break free.

Prayer: 1. I break the control of fear in my life, in Jesus' name.

2. I break free from limitations of fear, in Jesus' name.

DAY 36

It is written: "Then shalt thou prosper, if thou takest heed to fulfill the statutes and judgments which the LORD charged Moses with concerning Israel: be strong, and of good courage; dread not, nor be dismayed" (1 Chron. 22:13).

Principle: Fear makes you unsteady in the path of success.

Prayer:
1. O Lord God, restore me now to the path of success, in Jesus' name.
2. O Lord God, establish me in Your favor, in Jesus' name.

Day 37

It is written: "And David said to Solomon his son, 'Be strong and of good courage, and do it: fear not, nor be dismayed, for the LORD God, even my God, will be with thee; he will not fail thee, nor forsake thee, until thou hast finished all the work for the service of the house of the LORD'" (1 Chron. 28:20).

Principle: Fear keeps you back from finishing the good work, so just keep doing it.

Prayer: 1. In the name of Jesus, I break free from the spirit of non-accomplishment.

2. Henceforth, whatever good thing I begin, I shall gloriously finish, in Jesus' name.

Day 38

It is written: "Ye shall not need to fight in this battle: set yourselves, stand ye still, and see the salvation of the LORD with you, O Judah and Jerusalem: fear not, nor be dismayed; tomorrow go out against them: for the LORD will be with you (2 Chron. 20:17).

Principle: Fear prevents you from seeing victories around you.

Prayer:
1. I receive grace to stand firm and overcome fear, in Jesus' name.
2. I receive grace to be watchful for victories, in Jesus' name.

Day 39

It is written: "Then would I speak, and not fear him; but it is not so with me" (Job 9:35).

Principle: Fear may cost you your relationship with God.

Prayer:
1. Wounds caused by fear in my life, be healed now by the blood of Jesus, in Jesus' name.
2. Damage done to my life by fear, be repaired now, by the blood of Jesus, in Jesus' name.

Day 40

It is written: "If thou prepare thine heart, and stretch out thine hands toward him; if iniquity be in thine hand, put it far away, and let not wickedness dwell in thy tabernacles. For then shalt thou lift up thy face without spot; yea, thou shalt be steadfast, and shalt not fear" (Job 11:13-15).

Principle: Victory over sin and fear enhances a joyful countenance without shame.

Prayer:
1. I repent of my iniquity and receive forgiveness, in Jesus' name.
2. I command shame to depart from my life, in Jesus' name.

DAY 41

It is written: "He mocketh at fear, and is not affrighted; neither turneth he back from the sword" (Job 39:22).

Principle: Those who mock their fear would not be frightened by it.

Prayer: 1. Henceforth, I refuse to be mocked by fear, in Jesus' name.

2. I mock my fear and claim victory, in Jesus' name.

DAY 42

It is written: "Though a host should encamp against me, my heart shall not fear: though war should rise against me, in this will I be confident" (Ps. 27:3).

Principle: Evil encamps where fear abounds.

Prayer:
1. Whatever evil is encompassing me, flee now, in Jesus' name.
2. Presence of God Almighty, encompass me now, in Jesus' name.

Day 43

It is written: "Therefore will not we fear, though the earth be removed, and though the mountains be carried into the midst of the sea" (Ps. 46:2).

Principle: Changes around you should not make you fret; rather set your heart to expect the best.

Prayer: 1. I command obstacles to blessings in my life to give way now, in Jesus' name.

2. I command fear in my life to give way to peace now, in Jesus' name.

DAY 44

It is written: "In God I will praise his word, in God I have put my trust; I will not fear what flesh can do unto me" (Ps. 56:4).

Principle: Fear of man weakens your trust and praise of God.

Prayer:
1. My trust and confidence in God are restored, in Jesus' name.
2. I exalt God Almighty above the fear of men, in Jesus' name.

DAY 45

It is written: "And he led them on safely, so that they feared not: but the sea overwhelmed their enemies" (Ps. 78:53).

Principle: Those whom God keeps safe are forever free from fear.

Prayer: 1. Let my fear be covered up in the sea of forgetfulness, in Jesus' name.

2. O Lord God Almighty, keep me safe from fear, in Jesus' name.

Day 46

It is written: "The LORD is on my side; I will not fear: what can man do unto me?" (Ps. 118:6).

Principle: Assurance of God's presence secures you from fear.

Prayer:
1. Through the blood of Jesus, I subdue the fear of men in my life, in Jesus' name.
2. I withdraw my fear of men and surrender it to God Almighty, in Jesus' name.

Day 47

It is written: "Be not wise in thine own eyes: fear the LORD, and depart from evil. It shall be health to thy navel, and marrow to thy bones" (Prov. 3:7-8).

Principle: Resting on your own wisdom prevents renewal from God.

Prayer: 1. O Lord God, renew and refresh my wisdom in You, in Jesus' name.

2. I gain strength against my fear, in Jesus' name.

Day 48

It is written: "Be not wise in thine own eyes: fear the LORD, and depart from evil. It shall be health to thy navel, and marrow to thy bones" (Prov. 3:25-26).

Principle: Sudden fear takes away your confidence.

Prayer:
1. I prevail over sudden fear, in Jesus' name.
2. I gain back my confidence from sudden fear, which tries to capture it, in Jesus' name.

Day 49

It is written: "The fear of the LORD tendeth to life: and he that hath it shall abide satisfied; he shall not be visited with evil" (Prov. 19:23).

Principle: "Fear of the Lord gives life, security, and protection from harm" (NLT).

Prayer:
1. Evil visitation in my life through fear, depart to desolation now, in Jesus' name.
2. My security and protection from God be established now, in all areas of my life, in Jesus' name.

Day 50

It is written: "Let not thine heart envy sinners; but be thou in the fear of the LORD all the day long" (Prov. 23:17).

Principle: Reverencing God always keeps you from fear.

Prayer:
1. I renounce fear associated with envy in my life, in Jesus' name.
2. I receive grace to reverence God always, in Jesus' name.

DAY 51

It is written: "My son, fear thou the LORD and the king: and meddle not with them that are given to change: for their calamity shall rise suddenly; and who knoweth the ruin of them both?" (Prov. 24:21-22).

Principle: Meddling with the fearful makes both of you fall.

Prayer: 1. I renounce and break asunder any covenant of fear in my life, in Jesus' name.

2. Anointing of the Holy Spirit, destroy the yoke of fear in my life, in Jesus' name.

Day 52

It is written: "I know that, whatsoever God doeth, it shall be for ever: nothing can be put to it, nor any thing taken from it: and God doeth it, that men should fear before him" (Eccl. 3:14).

Principle: Everything God does will endure forever, that mankind may be in awe before Him.

Prayer:
1. Thank You, O God, for Your enduring work in my life, in Jesus' name.
2. I reverence Your holy name, O God, for Your marvelous work in my life, in Jesus' name.

Day 53

It is written: "And say unto him, 'Take heed, and be quiet; fear not, neither be faint-hearted for the two tails of these smoking firebrands, for the fierce anger of Rezin with Syria, and of the son of Remali'ah.' Thus saith the Lord GOD, 'It shall not stand, neither shall it come to pass'" (Isa. 7:4,7).

Principle: The purpose of fear is to invade your life and throw you into panic.

Prayer:
1. Thus says the Lord God of Hosts to any attack of fear in my life, "It shall not stand, neither shall it come to pass" (Isa. 7:7), in Jesus' name.
2. I command the invasion of fear into my life to cease, in Jesus' name.

Day 54

It is written: "The Lord has said to me in the strongest terms: Do not think like everyone else does. Do not be afraid that some plan conceived behind closed doors will be the end of you. Do not fear anything except the Lord Almighty. He alone is the Holy One. If you fear Him you need fear nothing else. He will keep you safe" (Isa. 8:11-14a NLT).

Principle: Only God Almighty alone can keep you safe from fear—trust Him.

Prayer:
1. Any evil plan conceived against me shall not prosper, in Jesus' name.
2. Thank You, God, for keeping me safe from fear, in Jesus' name.

Day 55

It is written: "Strengthen ye the weak hands, and confirm the feeble knees. Say to them that are of a fearful heart, 'Be strong, fear not: behold, your God will come with vengeance, even God with a recompense; he will come and save you'" (Isa. 35:3-4).

Principle: Fear makes you feeble and weak, but encouraging yourself in God strengthens your heart.

Prayer:
1. O Lord God, transform my weaknesses due to fear into strength, in Jesus' name.
2. I say no to a fearful heart, but yes to a sound mind, in Jesus' name.

Day 56

It is written: "Fear thou not; for I am with thee: be not dismayed; for I am thy God: I will strengthen thee; yea, I will help thee; yea, I will uphold thee with the right hand of my righteousness" (Isa. 41:10).

Principle: Help received from God upholds you against fear.

Prayer:
1. O Lord God, uphold me by Your Spirit against fear, in Jesus' name.
2. Strengthen my heart, O God, against fear, in Jesus' name.

Day 57

It is written: "For I the LORD thy God will hold thy right hand, saying unto thee, 'Fear not; I will help thee'" (Isa. 41:13).

Principle: Fear vanishes when God takes hold of you.

Prayer:
1. O Lord God, uphold me with Your right hand of righteousness, in Jesus' name.
2. Because the Lord God will help me, I shall not fear, in Jesus' name.

Day 58

It is written: "Fear not, thou worm Jacob, and ye men of Israel; I will help thee, saith the LORD, and thy Redeemer, the Holy One of Israel" (Isa. 41:14).

Principle: However despised you are because of fear, you can still be redeemed out of fear.

Prayer: 1. O Lord God, my Redeemer, redeem me out of fear, in Jesus' name.

2. I am fearless against my fear, in Jesus' name.

Day 59

It is written: "But now thus saith the LORD that created thee, O Jacob, and he that formed thee, O Israel, 'Fear not: for I have redeemed thee, I have called thee by thy name; thou art mine'" (Isa. 43:1).

Principle: Fear renders you helpless, but a personal touch from God restores confidence.

Prayer: 1. I have been created and formed by God without fear; therefore, I break free from fear, in Jesus' name.

2. Thank You, God Almighty, for redeeming me from fear, in Jesus' name.

Day 60

It is written: "Since thou wast precious in my sight, thou hast been honorable, and I have loved thee: therefore will I give men for thee, and people for thy life. Fear not; for I am with thee: I will bring thy seed from the east, and gather thee from the west: I will say to the north, 'Give up;' and to the south, 'Keep not back: bring my sons from far, and my daughters from the ends of the earth; even every one that is called by my name: for I have created him for my glory, I have formed him; yea, I have made him'" (Isa. 43:4-7).

Principle: Giving in to fear makes you feel less than you are.

Prayer:
1. I am precious, honorable, and loved, in Jesus' name.
2. May the spirit of fear be annulled in my life by the blood of Jesus, in the name of Jesus.

Day 61

It is written: "Thus saith the LORD that made thee, and formed thee from the womb, which will help thee; 'Fear not, O Jacob, my servant; and thou, Jesh'urun, whom I have chosen'" (Isa. 44:2).

Principle: Assured help strengthens against fear.

Prayer:
1. God, who formed me from the womb without fear, will surely make me live free of fear, in Jesus' name.
2. I decree to my life, be divinely assured against fear, in Jesus' name.

Day 62

It is written: "Fear ye not, neither be afraid: have not I told thee from that time, and have declared it? ye are even my witnesses. Is there a God besides me? Yea, there is no God; I know not any" (Isa. 44:8).

Principle: Fear makes you reluctant to stand as the true witness of God.

Prayer:
1. I am a living witness of God's greatness; therefore, I'm free from fear, in Jesus' name.
2. O Lord God Almighty, I declare that there is none like unto Thee in my life, in Jesus' name.

DAY 63

It is written: "Hearken unto me, ye that know righteousness, the people in whose heart is my law; fear ye not the reproach of men, neither be ye afraid of their revilings. For the moth shall eat them up like a garment, and the worm shall eat them like wool: but my righteousness shall be for ever, and my salvation from generation to generation" (Isa. 51:7-8).

Principle: Scorning, slanderous, and insulting talk may stricken you to fear—shun them.

Prayer:
1. Blood of Jesus, take away the reproach of fear from me, in Jesus' name.
2. I claim victory over the terror of fear, in Jesus' name.

Day 64

It is written: "Fear not; for thou shalt not be ashamed: neither be thou confounded; for thou shalt not be put to shame: for thou shalt forget the shame of thy youth, and shalt not remember the reproach of thy widowhood any more" (Isa. 54:4).

Principle: Fear is humiliating—permit it no longer.

Prayer:
1. O Lord God, lift me out of the humiliation of fear, in Jesus' name.
2. I break free from the cycle of shame, disgrace, and reproach, in Jesus' name.

Day 65

It is written: "In righteousness shalt thou be established: thou shalt be far from oppression; for thou shalt not fear: and from terror; for it shall not come near thee" (Isa. 54:14)

Principle: When fear takes root, oppression and terror result.

Prayer: 1. In the name of Jesus, I cast oppression and terror out of my life.

2. Henceforth, I'm free from oppressive fear, in Jesus' name.

Day 66

It is written: "No weapon that is formed against thee shall prosper; and every tongue that shall rise against thee in judgment thou shalt condemn. This is the heritage of the servants of the LORD, and their righteousness is of me, saith the LORD" (Isa. 54:14).

Principle: Fear is a destructive weapon; if it prevails, it may be deadly, so refute it.

Prayer:
1. Henceforth, no weapon of fear shall prosper in my life, in Jesus' name.
2. In the name of Jesus Christ, I condemn my fear.

Day 67

It is written: "Thine own wickedness shall correct thee, and thy backslidings shall reprove thee: know therefore and see that it is an evil thing and bitter, that thou hast forsaken the LORD thy God, and that my fear is not in thee, saith the Lord GOD of hosts" (Jer. 2:19).

Principle: Fear becomes evil and bitter when it makes you feel forsaken and rejected.

Prayer:
1. O Lord God, set me free from the bitterness of fear, in Jesus' name.
2. I overcome the bitter feelings of fear, in Jesus' name.

DAY 68

It is written: "Fear ye not me?" saith the LORD: "will ye not tremble at my presence, which have placed the sand for the bound of the sea by a perpetual decree, that it cannot pass it: and though the waves thereof toss themselves, yet can they not prevail; though they roar, yet can they not pass over it" (Jer. 2:19).

Principle: The waves of fear may toss and roar, but can never drown you. Keep believing.

Prayer:
1. I command the wave of fear set at me, be quenched, in Jesus' name.
2. I refuse the tossing and the roaring of fear in my life, in Jesus' name.

Day 69

It is written: "Forasmuch as there is none like unto thee, O LORD; thou art great, and thy name is great in might. Who would not fear thee, O King of nations? For to thee doth it appertain: forasmuch as among all the wise men of the nations, and in all their kingdoms, there is none like unto thee" (Jer. 10:6-7).

Principle: Declaring God's greatness expels your fear.

Prayer:
1. I declare that the Most High God is great in might, power, and majesty, in Jesus' name.
2. Almighty God, take all the glory of my life, in Jesus' name.

DAY 70

It is written: "Therefore fear thou not, O my servant Jacob," saith the LORD; "neither be dismayed, O Israel: for, lo, I will save thee from afar, and thy seed from the land of their captivity; and Jacob shall return, and shall be in rest, and be quiet, and none shall make him afraid" (Jer. 30:10).

Principle: Peace and security abound when you put your fears behind you.

Prayer:
1. According to Your Word, O God, "None shall make me afraid" (Jer. 30:10b), in Jesus' name.
2. O Lord God, give me rest from my fears, in Jesus' name.

Day 71

It is written: "And I will make an everlasting covenant with them, that I will not turn away from them, to do them good; but I will put my fear in their hearts, that they shall not depart from me" (Jer. 32:40).

Principle: Reverencing God in your heart is assurance of peace and security.

Prayer: 1. According to Your Word, O God, inspire me to reverence You always, in Jesus' name.

2. No fear shall stop me from being blessed, in Jesus' name.

DAY 72

It is written: "But fear not thou, O my servant Jacob, and be not dismayed, O Israel: for, behold, I will save thee from afar off, and thy seed from the land of their captivity; and Jacob shall return, and be in rest and at ease, and none shall make him afraid" (Jer. 46:27).

Principle: Fear threatens your peace and security, so stand strong.

Prayer:
1. I refuse to tremble for fear, in Jesus' name.
2. I overcome the threats of fear through the blood of Jesus, in Jesus' name.

Day 73

It is written: "Fear thou not, O Jacob my servant," saith the LORD: "for I am with thee; for I will make a full end of all the nations whither I have driven thee: but I will not make a full end of thee, but correct thee in measure; yet will I not leave thee wholly unpunished" (Jer. 46:28).

Principle: Evidence of a disciplined life is correcting the wrong caused by fear.

Prayer:
1. I receive grace to correct my wrongs, in Jesus' name.
2. O Lord God, let Your mercy annul every judgment upon my life, in Jesus' name.

Day 74

It is written: "I called upon thy name, O LORD, out of the low dungeon. Thou hast heard my voice: hide not thine ear at my breathing, at my cry. Thou drewest near in the day that I called upon thee thou saidst, Fear not" (Lam. 3:55-57).

Principle: A prayer cry is a victory cry against fear.

Prayer:
1. I thank You, God, for ever drawing near to me and attending to my cry, in Jesus' name.
2. O Lord God, make me hear Your comforting voice always, in Jesus' name.

DAY 75

It is written: "As an adamant harder than flint have I made thy forehead: fear them not, neither be dismayed at their looks, though they be a rebellious house" (Ezek. 3:9).

Principle: Looks are deceptive, don't be fearful by what you see or hear.

Prayer: 1. O God my Rock, defend me against my fears, in Jesus' name.

2. I prevail over every rebellious countenance, in Jesus' name.

Day 76

It is written: "Then said he unto me, 'Fear not, Daniel: for from the first day that thou didst set thine heart to understand, and to chasten thyself before thy God, thy words were heard, and I am come for thy words'" (Dan. 10:12).

Principle: Fear hinders answers to prayers.

Prayer:
1. Stronghold of fear hindering my answers to prayers, be taken away, in Jesus' name.
2. Answers to my prayers hindered by fear, come through by the mercies of God, in Jesus' name.

DAY 77

It is written: "O man greatly beloved, fear not: peace be unto thee; be strong, yea, be strong." And when he had spoken unto me, I was strengthened, and said, "Let my lord speak; for thou hast strengthened me" (Dan. 10:19).

Principle: God's love supersedes your fears and strengthens your soul.

Prayer:
1. I can boldly say that I am deeply loved by God; therefore, I am at peace, in Jesus' name.
2. O love of God, strengthen me against fear, in Jesus' name.

Day 78

It is written: "Fear not, O land; be glad and rejoice: for the LORD will do great things" (Joel 2:21).

Principle: Laugh at your fear. Sing rejoicingly to mock your fear.

Prayer: 1. I am glad, and I rejoice exceedingly because God Almighty has done great things for me, in Jesus' name.

2. Fear shall not hinder my miracles, in Jesus' name.

Day 79

It is written: "Be not afraid, ye beasts of the field: for the pastures of the wilderness do spring, for the tree beareth her fruit, the fig tree and the vine do yield their strength. Be glad then, ye children of Zion, and rejoice in the LORD your God: for he hath given you the former rain moderately, and he will cause to come down for you the rain, the former rain, and the latter rain in the first month" (Joel 2:22-23).

Principle: God's mercies are expressions of His love, so fear not.

Prayer:
1. I decree to everything within and around me, fear not! In Jesus' name.
2. I shall be fruitful in every good thing of life, and my fruits shall remain, in Jesus' name.

Day 80

It is written: "In that day it shall be said to Jerusalem, Fear thou not: and to Zion, Let not thine hands be slack" (Zeph. 3:16).

Principle: Fear brings slackness and slows you down; therefore, break free from fear.

Prayer:
1. Fear shall not keep me stagnant in life, in Jesus' name.
2. Fear shall no longer slow down my success in life, in Jesus' name.

DAY 81

It is written: "According to the word that I covenanted with you when ye came out of Egypt, so my Spirit remaineth among you: fear ye not" (Hag. 2:5).

Principle: Fear makes you feel you've lost it all, but be steadfast.

Prayer:
1. My covenant with God remains steadfast against fear, in Jesus' name.
2. The Spirit of the living God in me surpasses my fear, in Jesus' name.

Day 82

It is written: "And it shall come to pass, that as ye were a curse among the heathen, O house of Judah, and house of Israel; so will I save you, and ye shall be a blessing: fear not, but let your hands be strong" (Zech. 8:13).

Principle: Fear breeds curses, but faith in God stirs up blessings.

Prayer:
1. I command the curse of fear in my life to break asunder, in Jesus' name.
2. I receive the blessings of "fear not," in Jesus' name.

Day 83

It is written: "So again have I thought in these days to do well unto Jerusalem and to the house of Judah: fear ye not" (Zech. 8:15).

Principle: Fearful thoughts are as bad as expressed fear.

Prayer:
1. I pray my thoughts will be renewed in the Lord God Almighty, in Jesus' name.
2. Fear of wrong decisions shall not ruin my destiny, in Jesus' name.

Day 84

It is written: "But while he thought on these things, behold, the angel of the Lord appeared unto him in a dream, saying, Joseph, thou son of David, fear not to take unto thee Mary thy wife: for that which is conceived in her is of the Holy Ghost" (Matt. 1:20).

Principle: Fear does not recognize divine opportunities, so confidently take back good things fear has put away.

Prayer:
1. I take back my divine opportunities, in Jesus' name.
2. Henceforth, fear shall not hold me back from prospering, in Jesus' name.

DAY 85

It is written: "Fear them not therefore: for there is nothing covered, that shall not be revealed; and hid, that shall not be known" (Matt. 10:26).

Principle: Fear conceals a matter, but faith discloses it.

Prayer: 1. Holy Spirit, reveal the blessings fear has concealed in my life, in Jesus' name.

2. Fear shall no longer hide my blessings, in Jesus' name.

Day 86

It is written: "Fear ye not therefore, ye are of more value than many sparrows" (Matt. 10:31).

Principle: Fear conceals our worth and value, but faith reveals them.

Prayer:
1. My hidden value and worth, come forth now, in Jesus' name.
2. I break forth to celebrate my worth and value, in Jesus' name.

Day 87

> **It is written:** "And the angel answered and said unto the women, Fear not ye: for I know that ye seek Jesus, which was crucified" (Matt. 28:5).
>
> **Principle:** Fear makes you seek and never find, but a search of faith discovers the treasure.
>
> **Prayer:**
> 1. I shall never seek blessings in vain, in Jesus' name.
> 2. O Lord God, send Your angels to strengthen me against fear, in Jesus' name.

Day 88

It is written: "But the angel said unto him, Fear not, Zechari'ah: for thy prayer is heard; and thy wife Elisabeth shall bear thee a son, and thou shalt call his name John" (Luke 1:13).

Principle: Fear hinders prayer, but faith in God stirs up manifestations of His answers.

Prayer:
1. All hindrances to manifestation of answered prayers in my life be blotted out by the blood of Jesus, in Jesus' name.
2. Let all my delayed blessings manifest themselves now, in Jesus' name.

Day 89

It is written: "And the angel said unto her, Fear not, Mary: for thou hast found favor with God" (Luke 1:30).

Principle: Enjoying favor without fear multiplies the blessings.

Prayer:
1. O Lord God, favor my life with joyful testimonies, in Jesus' name.
2. O Lord God, overwhelm my life with Your favor, in Jesus' name.

Day 90

It is written: "And the angel said unto them, Fear not: for, behold, I bring you good tidings of great joy, which shall be to all people" (Luke 2:10).

Principle: Faith reassures against fear with good news.

Prayer:
1. O Lord God, send now Your angels to manifest good tidings in my life, in Jesus' name.
2. I receive good news with great joy, in Jesus' name.

DAY 91

It is written: "And so was also James, and John, the sons of Zeb'edee, which were partners with Simon. And Jesus said unto Simon, Fear not; from henceforth thou shalt catch men" (Luke 5:10).

Principle: Fear makes you prey, but faith makes you victorious.

Prayer:
1. I overcome the fear of men to disciple them to God's eternal kingdom, in Jesus' name.
2. I receive grace to win souls for God's kingdom, in Jesus' name.

Day 92

It is written: "But when Jesus heard it, he answered him, saying, Fear not: believe only, and she shall be made whole" (Luke 8:50).

Principle: Simply trust God, and keep trusting till your fear melts away.

Prayer:
1. Thank You, God Almighty, for healing me from fear and making me whole, in Jesus' name.
2. I believe, so I'm made whole, in Jesus' name.

DAY 93

It is written: "But even the very hairs of your head are all numbered. Fear not therefore: ye are of more value than many sparrows" (Luke 12:7).

Principle: Every part of me is precious and honorable and must be protected from fear.

Prayer: 1. Thank You, God Almighty, for watching over my life, in Jesus' name.

2. I am divinely protected from fear, in Jesus' name.

Day 94

It is written: "Fear not, little flock; for it is your Father's good pleasure to give you the kingdom" (Luke 12:32).

Principle: Age is no guarantee of fearlessness; fear could keep you from maturing.

Prayer:
1. I decree against the growth of fear in my life, in Jesus' name.
2. Fear shall not keep me from developing unto maturity, in Jesus' name.

Day 95

It is written: "Fear not, daughter of Zion: behold, thy King cometh, sitting on an ass's colt" (John 12:15).

Principle: Either fear rules you, or you rule over your fear.

Prayer:
1. Henceforth, I reign over my fear, in Jesus' name.
2. My Lord Jesus Christ, reign in Your fullness over my fear.

Day 96

It is written: "Fear not, Paul; thou must be brought before Caesar: and, lo, God hath given thee all them that sail with thee" (Acts 27:24).

Principle: Conquer your fear and stand before kings.

Prayer:
1. Fear shall not keep me in the valley; neither shall it keep me from inheriting the palace, in Jesus' name.
2. I command the storms and tempest of fear set before me to be quenched, in Jesus' name.

Day 97

It is written: "For ye have not received the spirit of bondage again to fear; but ye have received the Spirit of adoption, whereby we cry, Abba, Father" (Rom. 8:15).

Principle: Fear enslaves, therefore, break the chains in your mind.

Prayer:
1. I break the chains of fear in my mind, in Jesus' name.
2. I reject the spirit of fear and walk in freedom, in Jesus' name.

Day 98

It is written: "For God hath not given us the spirit of fear; but of power, and of love, and of a sound mind" (2 Tim. 1:7).

Principle: Fear is not a gift from God—reject it. But God's gifts empower you with a sound mind and overwhelm you with love.

Prayer:
1. O Lord God, empower me with a sound mind and overwhelm me with love, in Jesus' name.
2. I receive grace for self-discipline, in Jesus' name.

Day 99

It is written: "By faith he forsook Egypt, not fearing the wrath of the king: for he endured, as seeing him who is invisible" (Heb. 11:27).

Principle: Tolerating fear keeps you away from achieving your vision.

Prayer:
1. Wrath of fear against my life, be quenched, in Jesus' name.
2. I gain back my glorious visions that fear has prevented, in Jesus' name.

Day 100

It is written: "So that we may boldly say, The Lord is my helper, and I will not fear what man shall do unto me" (Heb. 13:6).

Principle: There's boldness against fear when God becomes your helper.

Prayer:
1. I claim boldness against my fear, in Jesus' name.
2. O Lord God, You're my helper; strengthen me against fear, in Jesus' name.

Day 101

It is written: "There is no fear in love; but perfect love casteth out fear: because fear hath torment. He that feareth is not made perfect in love" (1 John 4:18).

Principle: Fear torments and inflicts punishment and judgment on its victims.

Prayer:
1. I command the torment of fear in my life to cease, in Jesus' name.
2. The punishment and judgment of fear over my life, be terminated by the blood of Jesus, in Jesus' name.

Day 102

It is written: "And when I saw him, I fell at his feet as dead. And he laid his right hand upon me, saying unto me, Fear not; I am the first and the last" (Rev. 1:17).

Principle: Only God Almighty has the first and the last say, not fear.

Prayer:
1. O Lord God, revive me out of my fear, in Jesus' name.
2. God Almighty is my all in all; therefore, I shall not fear, in Jesus name.

Day 103

It is written: "Who shall not fear thee, O Lord, and glorify thy name? For thou only art holy: for all nations shall come and worship before thee; for thy judgments are made manifest" (Rev. 15:4).

Principle: Fear of God makes you glorify His name always.

Prayer:
1. I worship and glorify God Almighty for giving me victory over fear, in Jesus' name.
2. I exalt the lordship of Jesus Christ above all my fear, in Jesus' name.

Do Not Be Afraid

"Some of our fears are useful to us, but most of them are useless. If our useless fears had only a brief life span, we could tolerate them. The problem is that useless fears tend to hang on for years; some even follow us to the grave. It's not the fear that bothers us; it's the consequences of fear. A useful fear is one that prompts us to action in the face of a real threat."

—H. Norman Wright,
"Freedom From The Grip of Fear"

Day 104

It is written: "I will give peace in the land, and you shall lie down, and none will make you afraid; I will rid the land of evil beasts, and the sword will not go through your land" (Lev. 26:6).

Principle: Overwhelming peace makes you cease to fear.

Prayer:
1. I take refuge in God to rest from my fear, in Jesus' name.
2. Peace of God, overwhelm my life, in Jesus' name.

Day 105

It is written: "You shall not show partiality in judgment; you shall hear the small as well as the great; you shall not be afraid in any man's presence, for the judgment is God's. The case that is too hard for you, bring to me, and I will hear it" (Deut. 1:17).

Principle: Fear of man brings partiality in judgment, but judgment is God's.

Prayer:
1. I receive grace to discern and judge right, in Jesus' name.
2. Henceforth, I shall not be afraid of man's presence, but I will enjoy God's presence always, in Jesus' name.

Day 106

It is written: "Then I said to you, 'Do not be terrified, or afraid of them'" (Deut. 1:29).

Principle: Fear and terror are twin destroyers—conquer both.

Prayer: 1. In the name of Jesus, I conquer my fears and terror.

2. I refuse to be terrified with fear, in Jesus' name.

Day 107

It is written: "You shall not be afraid of them, but you shall remember well what the LORD your God did to Pharaoh and to all Egypt" (Deut. 7:18).

Principle: Memory of past exploits strengthens you against fear.

Prayer:
1. I testify of God's greatness against my fear, in Jesus' name.
2. I recall my past victories to overcome my present challenges, in Jesus' name.

DAY 108

It is written: "When a prophet speaks in the name of the LORD, if the thing does not happen or come to pass, that is the thing which the LORD has not spoken; the prophet has spoken it presumptuously; you shall not be afraid of him" (Deut. 18:22).

Principle: Fearful words spoken by men cannot stop you from attaining your goals.

Prayer: 1. I refute every fearful word ever spoken against me, in Jesus' name.

2. I press forward to attain my glorious goals in spite of fearful opposition, in Jesus' name.

Day 109

It is written: "When you go out to battle against your enemies, and see horses and chariots and people more numerous than you, do not be afraid of them; for the LORD your God is with you, who brought you up from the land of Egypt" (Deut. 20:1).

Principle: Multitude of people, however strongly arrayed for war, cannot stop you from fulfilling your goals.

Prayer:
1. Multiple oppositions against my life shall not prevail, in Jesus' name.
2. The Lord God is with me, who has brought me out of the bondage of fear, in Jesus' name.

Day 110

It is written: "Have I not commanded you? Be strong and of good courage; do not be afraid, nor be dismayed, for the LORD your God is with you wherever you go" (Josh. 1:9).

Principle: Never permit fear to discourage you from progressing in your goals.

Prayer:
1. I am strong and of good courage and never give in to dismay, in Jesus' name.
2. Wherever I go, I'm fearless against fear, in Jesus' name.

Day 111

It is written: "But the LORD said to Joshua, 'Do not be afraid because of them, for tomorrow about this time I will deliver all of them slain before Israel. You shall hamstring their horses and burn their chariots with fire'" (Josh. 11:6).

Principle: Your fear today, if properly challenged, cannot survive tomorrow.

Prayer:
1. I cripple the horses of fear and burn their chariots, in Jesus' name.
2. I confront my fear of today for a better tomorrow, in Jesus' name.

DAY 112

It is written: "And the angel of the LORD said to Elijah, 'Go down with him; do not be afraid of him.' So he arose and went down with him to the king" (2 Kings 1:15).

Principle: Arising out of your fear brings you before kings.

Prayer:
1. I refuse to be summoned to fear and bondage, in Jesus' name.
2. I arise out of my fear to stand before kings, in Jesus' name.

DAY 113

It is written: "But they were exceedingly afraid, and said, 'Look, two kings could not stand up to him; how then can we stand?'" (2 Kings 10:4).

Principle: Never be paralyzed with fear; at your best, fear cannot stand you.

Prayer: 1. Fear attacks cannot hold me bound anymore, in Jesus' name.

2. Joy of the Lord, replace my fears, in Jesus' name.

Day 114

It is written: "And Isaiah said to them, 'Thus you shall say to your master, "Thus says the LORD: 'Do not be afraid of the words which you have heard, with which the servants of the king of Assyria have blasphemed Me. Surely I will send a spirit upon him, and he shall hear a rumor and return to his own land; and I will cause him to fall by the sword in his own land.'"'" (2 Kings 19:6-7).

Principle: Fear blasphemes against the truth—do not get caught with it.

Prayer:
1. I refute every blasphemy against the truth, in Jesus' name.
2. I receive grace to embrace the truth, in Jesus' name.

DAY 115

It is written: "And Gedaliah took an oath before them and their men, and said to them, 'Do not be afraid of the servants of the Chaldeans. Dwell in the land and serve the king of Babylon, and it shall be well with you'" (2 Kings 25:24).

Principle: Fear enslaves princes and makes the inferior rule over the superior.

Prayer:
1. I shall dwell in the land of the living without fear and terror, in Jesus' name.
2. It shall be well with me and my household in the land of the living, in Jesus' name.

Day 116

It is written: "And he said, 'Listen, all you of Judah and you inhabitants of Jerusalem, and you, King Jehoshaphat! Thus says the LORD to you: "Do not be afraid nor dismayed because of this great multitude, for the battle is not yours, but God's"'" (2 Chron. 20:15).

Principle: Battling your fears alone may be difficult; trust God for strength.

Prayer:
1. Hear, O my fears, the battle is not mine, but God's, so I claim the victories, in Jesus' name.
2. I turn my battles against fear over to God Almighty and I possess my victories, in Jesus' name.

DAY 117

It is written: "Be strong and courageous; do not be afraid nor dismayed before the king of Assyria, nor before all the multitude that is with him; for there are more with us than with him" (2 Chron. 32:7).

Principle: You are stronger than your fears—be courageous.

Prayer:
1. I am strong and courageous; therefore, I'll not be dismayed, in Jesus' name.
2. Angels of the living God, reinforce Your presence in my life against fear, in Jesus' name.

Day 118

It is written: "Therefore the king said to me, 'Why is your face sad, since you are not sick? This is nothing but sorrow of heart.' So I became dreadfully afraid" (Neh. 2:2).

Principle: Fear results in sorrow of heart and makes the face sad.

Prayer:
1. I refute the sorrow of heart and a sad countenance, in Jesus' name.
2. Holy Spirit, gladden my heart for a brighter countenance, in Jesus' name.

Day 119

It is written: "And I looked, and arose and said to the nobles, to the leaders, and to the rest of the people, 'Do not be afraid of them. Remember the Lord, great and awesome, and fight for your brethren, your sons, your daughters, your wives, and your houses'" (Neh. 4:14).

Principle: Fear can invade families and make the homes dreadful and difficult for habitation.

Prayer:
1. O Lord God, fight and defend my family from troubles, in Jesus' name.
2. In the name of Jesus, fear shall not be able to invade my family.

Day 120

It is written: "For they all were trying to make us afraid, saying, 'Their hands will be weakened in the work, and it will not be done'" (Neh. 6:9).

Principle: Fear weakens your hands from accomplishing success—cry out for strength.

Prayer: 1. Now therefore, O God, strengthen my hands, in Jesus' name.

2. My hands shall not be weakened or unable to achieve success, in Jesus' name.

Day 121

It is written: "You shall be hidden from the scourge of the tongue, And you shall not be afraid of destruction when it comes" (Job 5:21).

Principle: Fear scourges and the pains are dreadful—seek protection.

Prayer:
1. O Lord God, protect me from the scourging of fear, in Jesus' name.
2. Blood of Jesus, set me free from the pains of fear, in Jesus' name.

Day 122

It is written: "You shall laugh at destruction and famine, And you shall not be afraid of the beasts of the earth" (Job 5:22).

Principle: Fear is a mocker—laugh at it before it destroys you.

Prayer:
1. I laugh my fear to scorn, in Jesus' name.
2. I silence the mockery of fear in my life, in Jesus' name.

Day 123

It is written: "For now you are nothing, You see terror and are afraid" (Job 6:21).

Principle: Helpers are helpless when faced with fear.

Prayer: 1. O Lord, send profitable helpers to bless me, in Jesus' name.

2. O Lord God, strengthen my helpers to help me, in Jesus' name.

Day 124

It is written: "If I say, 'I will forget my complaint, I will put off my sad face and wear a smile,' I am afraid of all my sufferings; I know that You will not hold me innocent" (Job 9:27-28).

Principle: Fear increases complaints and heaviness of heart—smile it off.

Prayer: 1. I receive grace to overcome complaints and murmuring, in Jesus' name.

2. I escape the sufferings of fear and turn to joy, in Jesus' name.

Day 125

It is written: "So Elihu, the son of Barachel the Buzite, answered and said: 'I am young in years, and you are very old; Therefore I was afraid, And dared not declare my opinion to you'" (Job 32:6).

Principle: Wisdom against fear is a divine endowment regardless of age.

Prayer:
1. O Lord God, endue me with wisdom against my fear, in Jesus' name.
2. I break free from fear limitations, in Jesus' name.

Day 126

It is written: "I will not be afraid of ten thousands of people who have set themselves against me all around" (Ps. 3:6).

Principle: Encompassing fear should not intimidate you; rather, it celebrates your success while you rejoice over its defeat.

Prayer: 1. Fear encompassing my life, celebrate now my success because you've lost your dread, in Jesus' name.

2. Peace and joy, encompass me now, in Jesus' name.

DAY 127

It is written: "Do not be afraid when one becomes rich, When the glory of his house is increased; For when he dies he shall carry nothing away; His glory shall not descend after him" (Ps. 49:16-17).

Principle: Someone else's better fortune should not arouse your fear—check yourself and rejoice with him.

Prayer:
1. I bind and cast the spirit of envy out of my life, in Jesus' name.
2. O Lord God, make me to discover my glorious fortune, in Jesus' name.

Day 128

It is written: "In God I have put my trust; I will not be afraid. What can man do to me?" (Ps. 56:11).

Principle: Trust in God gives confidence against the boasting of men.

Prayer:
1. I boast of God's greatness and I'm thankful for His goodness in my life, in Jesus' name.
2. I proclaim that the boasting of men in my life shall cease, in Jesus' name.

Day 129

It is written: "You shall not be afraid of the terror by night, Nor of the arrow that flies by day" (Ps. 91:5).

Principle: Fear brings terror by night and day, but you can escape.

Prayer:
1. Terror and arrows of fear, flee from my life, in Jesus' name.
2. Blood of Jesus, shield me from the terror and arrows of fear, in Jesus' name.

Day 130

It is written: "He will not be afraid of evil tidings; His heart is steadfast, trusting in the LORD" (Ps. 112:7).

Principle: Bad news creates fear, but good news refreshes the soul.

Prayer:
1. All bad news and its consequences for me, through the blood of Jesus, turn to blessings, in Jesus' name.
2. I bind and cast out fear of bad news from my life, in Jesus' name.

Day 131

It is written: "His heart is established; He will not be afraid, Until he sees his desire upon his enemies" (Ps. 112:8).

Principle: Those who are confident and fearless can face their foes triumphantly.

Prayer: 1. I boldly confess that I'm confident and fearless of enemies' attacks, because they are defeated and I'm victorious, in Jesus' name.

2. In the name of Jesus, I break the confidence of my adversaries.

Day 132

It is written: "When you lie down, you will not be afraid; Yes, you will lie down and your sleep will be sweet" (Prov. 3:24).

Principle: "You can lie down without fear and enjoy pleasant dreams" (NLT).

Prayer:
1. I refute every dream attack and annul the consequences by the blood of Jesus, in Jesus' name.
2. I welcome God's participation in my dream life, in Jesus' name.

Day 133

It is written: "Do not be afraid of sudden terror, Nor of trouble from the wicked when it comes; for the LORD will be your confidence, And will keep your foot from being caught" (Prov. 3:25-26).

Principle: Fear traps are destructive, but you can confidently escape from them.

Prayer:
1. I break free and break loose from fear traps, in Jesus' name.
2. God Almighty is my security against fear traps, in Jesus' name.

Day 134

It is written: "She is not afraid of snow for her household, For all her household is clothed with scarlet" (Prov. 31:21).

Principle: Keep yourself warm from the stormy wind of fear.

Prayer:
1. Holy Spirit's fire, warm me up against the sudden storm of fear, in Jesus' name.
2. O Lord God, shield me with Your divine presence, in Jesus' name.

Day 135

It is written: "Therefore thus says the Lord GOD of hosts: "O My people, who dwell in Zion, do not be afraid of the Assyrian. He shall strike you with a rod and lift up his staff against you, in the manner of Egypt. For yet a very little while and the indignation will cease, as will My anger in their destruction""" (Isa. 10:24-25).

Principle: Fear smites with great wrath, but it can be turned away.

Prayer:
1. O Lord God, turn away the wrath of fear from my life, in Jesus' name.
2. Every rage of fear against my life, be turned away to desolation, in Jesus' name.

DAY 136

It is written: "Behold, God is my salvation; I will trust and not be afraid: 'for the LORD JEHOVAH is my strength and song; He also is become my salvation'" (Isa. 12:2).

Principle: Singing and making melody in the face of fear dispel your fear.

Prayer: 1. My inner man, sing for joy evermore, in Jesus' name.

2. I rejoice over my defeat of fear forever, in Jesus' name.

DAY 137

It is written: "For thus the LORD has spoken to me: 'As a lion roars, And a young lion over his prey (when a multitude of shepherds is summoned against him, He will not be afraid of their voice nor be disturbed by their noise), so the LORD of hosts will come down to fight for Mount Zion and for its hill. Like birds flying about, so will the LORD of hosts defend Jerusalem. Defending, He will also deliver it; Passing over, He will preserve it'" (Isa. 31:4-5).

Principle: Multiple voices of fear can be so confusing—be not frightened.

Prayer:
1. Voice of the Lord God Almighty, silence the multiple voices of fear in my life, in Jesus' name.
2. O Lord God, let Your divine presence hover over my life, in Jesus' name.

Day 138

It is written: "And Isaiah said to them, 'Thus you shall say to your master, "Thus says the LORD: 'Do not be afraid of the words which you have heard, with which the servants of the king of Assyria have blasphemed Me'"'" (Isa. 37:6)

Principle: Blasphemous words are fearful words that disturb the soul.

Prayer: 1. Holy Spirit, lift up your standard against blasphemous words set at me, in Jesus' name.

2. Holy Spirit, shield me from attacks of blasphemous words, in Jesus' name.

Day 139

It is written: "O Zion, You who bring good tidings, Get up into the high mountain; O Jerusalem, You who bring good tidings, Lift up your voice with strength, Lift it up, be not afraid; Say to the cities of Judah, 'Behold your God!'" (Isa. 40:9).

Principle: Fear may be a silent killer or a shouting oppressor—whichever way it appears, conquer it.

Prayer:
1. I command every fear manipulation on my life to cease, in Jesus' name.
2. I conquer fear of the unknown, in Jesus' name.

Day 140

It is written: "'Do not be afraid of their faces, For I am with you to deliver you,' says the LORD" (Jer. 1:8).

Principle: Fear hinders you from fulfilling divine assignments—contend against it.

Prayer:
1. Fear shall not hinder me from fulfilling my divine assignments, in Jesus' name.
2. I receive grace to fulfill my divine assignments, in Jesus' name.

DAY 141

It is written: "They are upright, like a palm tree, And they cannot speak; They must be carried, Because they cannot go by themselves. Do not be afraid of them, For they cannot do evil, Nor can they do any good" (Jer. 10:5).

Principle: Fear can be harmful and render you helpless, yet you can overpower it.

Prayer:
1. I am not afraid, neither am I fearful because Jesus Christ is the Lord of my life, in Jesus' name.
2. The hurting caused by fear in my life, be cured by the blood of Jesus, in Jesus' name.

Day 142

It is written: "But I will deliver you in that day," says the LORD, "and you shall not be given into the hand of the men of whom you are afraid" (Jer. 39:17).

Principle: "But I will rescue you from those you fear so much … ." (NLT).

Prayer:
1. O Lord God, rescue me from those whom I feared greatly, in Jesus' name.
2. I receive grace to love and appreciate people, and I am free from fear, in Jesus' name.

DAY 143

It is written: "Do not be afraid of the king of Babylon, of whom you are afraid; do not be afraid of him," says the LORD, "for I am with you, to save you and deliver you from his hand" (Jer. 42:11).

Principle: You can be saved and rescued from the grip of fear.

Prayer:
1. O Lord God, save and rescue me from the grip of fearful ones, in Jesus' name.
2. Thank You, God Almighty, for rescuing me from all fearful attacks, in Jesus' name.

Day 144

It is written: "And you, son of man, do not be afraid of them nor be afraid of their words, though briers and thorns are with you and you dwell among scorpions; do not be afraid of their words or dismayed by their looks, though they are a rebellious house" (Ezek. 2:6).

Principle: Attacks of fear may be as sharp as thorns and sting like scorpions—quench the attacks.

Prayer:
1. In the name of Jesus, I command the flaming darts of fear against my life to be quenched.
2. Arrows of fear, depart from my life, in Jesus' name.

Day 145

It is written: "And although he wanted to put him to death, he feared the multitude, because they counted him as a prophet" (Matt. 14:27).

Principle: You can walk on your fear and trample hard on it to the point of no recovery.

Prayer:
1. I tread down my fears, in Jesus' name.
2. Fear shall not put me under, but I put it under, in Jesus' name.

Day 146

It is written: "But Jesus came and touched them and said, 'Arise, and do not be afraid'" (Matt. 17:7).

Principle: Do not permit fear to give you a false identity—rather, be transformed in your mind.

Prayer: 1. Thus says the Lord God unto me, "Arise, and do not be afraid," in Jesus' name.

2. Holy Spirit, transform me gloriously from inside out, in Jesus' name.

DAY 147

It is written: "Then Jesus said to them, 'Do not be afraid. Go and tell My brethren to go to Galilee, and there they will see Me'" (Matt. 28:10).

Principle: Proclaim and celebrate your freedom from fear daily.

Prayer:
1. In the name of Jesus, I proclaim and celebrate my freedom from fear.
2. I decree my freedom from fear to be permanent, in Jesus' name.

DAY 148

It is written: "As soon as Jesus heard the word that was spoken, He said to the ruler of the synagogue, 'Do not be afraid; only believe'" (Mark 5:36).

Principle: Do not trust your fear, but trust God only.

Prayer: 1. The dread of fear has lost hold on me, in Jesus' name.

2. I believe, Lord. Help me out of fear, in Jesus' name.

Day 149

It is written: "For they all saw Him and were troubled. But immediately He talked with them and said to them, 'Be of good cheer! It is I; do not be afraid'" (Mark 6:50).

Principle: Fear makes you scream in terror from a sense of danger—rather, cry out to God for help.

Prayer: 1. I bear no more the sense of danger, but of safety and peace, in Jesus' name.

2. O God, I call out for help and comfort. Help me, in Jesus' name.

Day 150

It is written: "Because he did not know what to say, for they were greatly afraid" (Mark 9:6).

Principle: Fear at times leaves you not knowing what to say, so rebuke it.

Prayer: 1. O Lord God, give me a word in season against fear, in Jesus' name.

2. I refuse to be muzzled by fear, in Jesus' name.

Day 151

It is written: "But they did not understand this saying, and were afraid to ask Him" (Mark 9:32).

Principle: Fear sometimes prevents you from asking the right questions.

Prayer: 1. O God, make me ask rightly and position me to receive, in Jesus' name.

2. I shall not be fearful to ask profitable questions, in Jesus' name.

Day 152

It is written: "So they went out quickly and fled from the tomb, for they trembled and were amazed. And they said nothing to anyone, for they were afraid" (Mark 16:8).

Principle: Do not ever permit fear to keep you from sharing the good news.

Prayer: 1. I shall not tremble, neither will I be terrified to share the good news of the kingdom, in Jesus' name.

2. Lord God, empower me to share Your good news with mankind, in Jesus' name.

DAY 153

It is written: "And I say to you, My friends, do not be afraid of those who kill the body, and after that have no more that they can do" (Luke 12:4).

Principle: Fear is destructive and, worst still, it can destroy the spirit.

Prayer:
1. I decree to my life that no fear can kill me in body, soul or spirit, in Jesus' name.
2. Fear shall not be able to destroy my destiny, in Jesus' name.

DAY 154

It is written: "But He said to them, 'It is I; do not be afraid.' Then they willingly received Him into the boat, and immediately the boat was at the land where they were going" (John 6:20-21).

Principle: Willingness and eagerness to journey with Jesus make you reach your shore of God's plan for your life.

Prayer:
1. Lord Jesus Christ, I invite You to journey with me in this world and the world to come, in Jesus' name.
2. I shall reach my shore of God's plan for my life, in Jesus' name.

DAY 155

It is written: "Let not your heart be troubled; you believe in God, believe also in Me" (John 14:1).

Principle: A troubled heart is a distrusting heart—keep trusting God.

Prayer: 1. O Lord God, heal my troubled heart, in Jesus' name.

2. My heart, be troubled no more, in Jesus' name.

Day 156

It is written: "Peace I leave with you, My peace I give to you; not as the world gives do I give to you. Let not your heart be troubled, neither let it be afraid" (John 14:27).

Principle: Peace of mind and heart is a gift from God—ask and you shall receive.

Prayer: 1. O Lord God, I ask and receive the gift of peace of mind and heart, in Jesus' name.

2. Peace of God, rule my life, in Jesus' name.

Day 157

It is written: "And when Saul had come to Jerusalem, he tried to join the disciples; but they were all afraid of him, and did not believe that he was a disciple" (Acts 9:26).

Principle: Fear of rejection could ensnare progress—constantly refute it.

Prayer: 1. I am accepted by God for favor and blessings, in Jesus' name.

2. I overcome rejection through the blood of Jesus, in Jesus' name.

DAY 158

It is written: "Then Crispus, the ruler of the synagogue, believed on the Lord with all his household. And many of the Corinthians, hearing, believed and were baptized. Now the Lord spoke to Paul in the night by a vision, 'Do not be afraid, but speak, and do not keep silent'" (Acts 18:9-10).

Principle: Never allow fear to discontinue your flow of uncommon opportunities.

Prayer:
1. My flow of uncommon opportunities shall not cease, in Jesus' name.
2. There shall be no discontinuity of blessing in my life, in Jesus' name.

Day 159

It is written: "And those who were with me indeed saw the light and were afraid, but they did not hear the voice of Him who spoke to me" (Acts 22:9).

Principle: Fear can prevent you from both seeing and hearing glorious opportunities.

Prayer:
1. I receive grace to see and hear glorious things, in Jesus' name.
2. I decree to my senses, be awakened to Your miracles, in Jesus' name.

Day 160

It is written: "For rulers are not a terror to good works, but to evil. Do you want to be unafraid of the authority? Do what is good, and you will have praise from the same. For he is God's minister to you for good. But if you do evil, be afraid; for he does not bear the sword in vain; for he is God's minister, an avenger to execute wrath on him who practices evil. Therefore you must be subject, not only because of wrath but also for conscience' sake" (Rom. 13:3-5).

Principle: You are profiting when you get along well with authorities with a clear conscience and without fear.

Prayer:
1. I bless the rulers of nations with peace and wisdom, in Jesus' name.
2. I bless the government of the nations of the world with the fear of the Lord, in Jesus' name.

Day 161

It is written: "By faith Moses, when he was born, was hidden three months by his parents, because they saw he was a beautiful child; and they were not afraid of the king's command" (Heb. 11:23).

Principle: Fearlessly defend your life against corruption, and be thankful.

Prayer:
1. I am a child of glorious destiny; therefore, I shall not die unfulfilled, in Jesus' name.
2. I fearlessly decree against destroyers of my God-ordained destiny; they shall not prevail against my life, in Jesus' name.

Day 162

It is written: "As Sarah obeyed Abraham, calling him lord, whose daughters you are if you do good and are not afraid with any terror" (1 Pet. 3:6).

Principle: Doing good without fear and terror are sure ways of retaining your heritage.

Prayer:
1. Henceforth, I shall fearlessly do good without being terrified, in Jesus' name.
2. Good works shall proceed from my life henceforth, in Jesus' name.

Day 163

It is written: "But even if you should suffer for righteousness' sake, you are blessed. And do not be afraid of their threats, nor be troubled" (1 Pet. 3:14).

Principle: Suffering for doing what is right should not make you fret. Keep doing it, for there is a reward.

Prayer: 1. I shall possess my reward for doing right things, in Jesus' name.

2. I shall fearlessly pursue doing what is right and never give up, in Jesus' name.

BE NOT TERRIFIED
BE NOT ANXIOUS
DREAD NOT
COURAGE

"It has been well said that our anxiety does not empty tomorrow of its sorrows, but it only empties today of its strength."

—Charles H. Spurgeon

Day 164

It is written: "Then I said to you, 'Do not be terrified, or afraid of them'" (Deut. 1:29).

Principle: No terror or fear should keep you from success in life.

Prayer:
1. I refuse to be terrified, in Jesus' name.
2. I despise the terror of oppressors, in Jesus' name.

DAY 165

It is written: "You shall not be terrified of them; for the LORD your God, the great and awesome God, is among you" (Deut. 7:21).

Principle: My fears are no fear to God Almighty, neither are my dreads; for He's an awesome God.

Prayer: 1. I turn my fears and dreads over to God Almighty, and I remain fearless, in Jesus' name.

2. O Lord God, let Your awesomeness beautify my life, in Jesus' name.

Day 166

It is written: "But when you hear of wars and commotions, do not be terrified; for these things must come to pass first, but the end will not come immediately" (Luke 21:9).

Principle: Wars and commotions are signs of the end time—don't be afraid.

Prayer: 1. Wars and commotions shall not be able to consume me, in Jesus' name.

2. Holy Spirit, equip me for success in this end of the age, in Jesus' name.

DAY 167

It is written: "And not in any way terrified by your adversaries, which is to them a proof of perdition, but to you of salvation, and that from God" (Phil. 1:28).

Principle: "Don't be intimidated by your enemies. This will be a sign to them that they are going to be destroyed, but that you are going to be saved, even by God himself" (NLT).

Prayer: 1. I refute the intimidation of my oppressors, in Jesus' name.

2. O God, save me by Your strength, in Jesus' name.

Day 168

It is written: "But as for your donkeys that were lost three days ago, do not be anxious about them, for they have been found. And on whom is all the desire of Israel? Is it not on you and on all your father's house?" (1 Sam. 9:20).

Principle: Fearlessly seeking what is lost may lead to the discovery of abandoned blessing.

Prayer:
1. O God, search and recover all my lost virtues, in Jesus' name.
2. I fearlessly record all my lost blessings, in Jesus' name.

Day 169

It is written: "Thus says the LORD: 'Cursed is the man who trusts in man and makes flesh his strength, Whose heart departs from the LORD. For he shall be like a shrub in the desert, And shall not see when good comes, But shall inhabit the parched places in the wilderness, In a salt land which is not inhabited. "Blessed is the man who trusts in the LORD, And whose hope is the LORD. For he shall be like a tree planted by the waters, which spreads out its roots by the river, And will not fear when heat comes; But its leaf will be green, and will not be anxious in the year of drought, Nor will cease from yielding fruit'" (Jer. 17:5-8).

Principle: Trusting God with all your heart releases grace to relate with mankind.

Prayer:
1. God Almighty, forgive me for not trusting You enough, in Jesus' name.
2. I receive grace to trust God wholeheartedly, in Jesus' name.

Day 170

It is written: "Then He said to His disciples, 'Therefore I say to you, do not worry about your life, what you will eat; nor about the body, what you will put on. Life is more than food, and the body is more than clothing. Consider the ravens, for they neither sow nor reap, which have neither storehouse nor barn; and God feeds them. Of how much more value are you than the birds? And which of you by worrying can add one cubit to his stature? If you then are not able to do the least, why are you anxious for the rest? Consider the lilies, how they grow: they neither toil nor spin; and yet I say to you, even Solomon in all his glory was not arrayed like one of these. If then God so clothes the grass, which today is in the field and tomorrow is thrown into the oven, how much more will He clothe you, O you of little faith? And do not seek what you should eat or what you should drink, nor have an anxious mind'" (Luke 12:22-29).

Principle: Breaking the cycle of worry, doubt, and fear reassures you of a better tomorrow.

Prayer:
1. By the blood of Jesus, I break the cycle of worry, doubt, and fear in my life, in Jesus' name.
2. Holy Spirit, strength me against worry, doubt, and fear, in Jesus' name.

Day 171

It is written: "Be anxious for nothing, but in everything by prayer and supplication, with thanksgiving, let your requests be made known to God" (Phil. 4:6).

Principle: Be specific about your needs when you pray, and be thankful.

Prayer: 1. I'm anxious for nothing, but shall ever be grateful unto God, in Jesus' name.

2. I receive a calm, well-balanced and disciplined mind, in Jesus' name.

Day 172

It is written: "And my God shall supply all your need according to His riches in glory by Christ Jesus" (Phil. 4:19).

Principle: Fear of not getting your needs met may cripple you, but rest assured that God will liberally supply and fill to the full your every need, to His glory.

Prayer:
1. Thank You, God Almighty, for being my all in all, in Jesus' name.
2. I'm open to receive divine supply, in Jesus' name.

Day 173

It is written: "I can do all things through Christ who strengthens me" (Phil. 4:13).

Principle: When God empowers, you'll be ready for anything and equal to anything till success is achieved.

Prayer:
1. I am self-sufficient in Christ's sufficiency, in Jesus' name.
2. Thank You, my Lord Jesus, for infusing Your inner strength into me, in Jesus' name.

Day 174

It is written: "Rejoice in the Lord always. Again I will say, rejoice!" (Phil. 4:4).

Principle: Rejoicing in God Almighty always assures you of unlimited victories.

Prayer: 1. I delight in Your awesome presence, O God, fill me now with Your glory, in Jesus' name.

2. O God, I open up my life to You. Fill me with Your joyful presence, in Jesus' name.

Day 175

It is written: "For it is God who works in you both to will and to do for His good pleasure" (Phil. 2:13).

Principle: Conquering fear takes the will and power to stand confidently when shaken by it.

Prayer: 1. Thank You, O God, for granting me the will and the power to conquer my fears, in Jesus' name.

2. O Lord God, work in me by Your Spirit to overcome my fears, in Jesus' name.

DAY 176

It is written: "Being confident of this very thing, that He who has begun a good work in you will complete it until the day of Jesus Christ" (Phil. 1:6).

Principle: Continuing in good works and developing them to fullness in spite of fearful attacks, establishes you as a champion.

Prayer:
1. O Lord God, perform Your good works in all areas of my life, in Jesus' name.
2. I receive grace to bring to completion every good thing ordained for my life, in Jesus' name.

Day 177

It is written: "Therefore God also has highly exalted Him and given Him the name which is above every name, that at the name of Jesus every knee should bow, of those in heaven, and of those on earth, and of those under the earth, and that every tongue should confess that Jesus Christ is Lord, to the glory of God the Father" (Phil. 2:9-11).

Principle: The strongest attack of fear cannot bring me low, because Jesus Christ is my all in all.

Prayer: 1. I command fear to bow before me, in Jesus' name.

2. I confess Jesus Christ as Lord over all my fears, in Jesus' name.

Day 178

It is written: "Finally, brethren, whatever things are true, whatever things are noble, whatever things are just, whatever things are pure, whatever things are lovely, whatever things are of good report, if there is any virtue and if there is anything praiseworthy—meditate on these things. The things which you learned and received and heard and saw in me, these do, and the God of peace will be with you" (Phil. 4:8-9).

Principle: Model your way of living after God and you will be undisturbed by fear.

Prayer:
1. O God of peace, manifest Your greatness in my life, in Jesus' name.
2. Fear shall not pierce my life because of the Holy Spirit of God, in Jesus' name.

Day 179

It is written: "Do all things without complaining and disputing, that you may become blameless and harmless, children of God without fault in the midst of a crooked and perverse generation, among whom you shine as lights in the world" (Phil. 2:14-15).

Principle: Faultfinding when attacked by fear deepens the bondage.

Prayer:
1. I repent of my faultfinding. O God, forgive me, in Jesus' name.
2. Power to prevail over grumbling and doubting, I receive, in Jesus' name.

Day 180

It is written: "Now to Him who is able to keep you from stumbling, And to present you faultless Before the presence of His glory with exceeding joy ...." (Jude 24).

Principle: Fear can make you stumble, slip, and fall unto condemnation—triumph over it.

Prayer: 1. I refuse to stumble, slip, and fall into condemnation, in Jesus' name.

2. Thank You, Lord God Almighty, for You're more than able to keep me from falling, in Jesus' name.

DAY 181

It is written: "Only be strong and very courageous, that you may observe to do according to all the law which Moses My servant commanded you; do not turn from it to the right hand or to the left, that you may prosper wherever you go" (Josh. 1:7).

Principle: Courage to obey God is victory over fear.

Prayer:
1. Henceforth, I shall manifest courage to obey God, in Jesus' name.
2. Courage not to turn away from the truth, I receive, in Jesus' name.

Day 182

It is written: "Therefore be very courageous to keep and to do all that is written in the Book of the Law of Moses, lest you turn aside from it to the right hand or to the left" (Josh. 23:6).

Principle: Courage to keep and do God's will provides victory.

Prayer:
1. I shall not turn away from the truth of God's Word, in Jesus' name.
2. O Lord God, empower me to walk in the truth of Your Word, in Jesus' name.

Day 183

It is written: "Then you will prosper, if you take care to fulfill the statutes and judgments with which the LORD charged Moses concerning Israel. Be strong and of good courage; do not fear nor be dismayed" (1 Chron. 22:13).

Principle: Never lose heart in your struggle against fear.

Prayer: 1. I refuse to lose heart in my struggle against fear, in Jesus' name.

2. I am courageous, therefore, I dread not, neither am I dismayed, in Jesus' name.

Day 184

It is written: "And take notice: Amariah the chief priest is over you in all matters of the LORD; and Zebadiah the son of Ishmael, the ruler of the house of Judah, for all the king's matters; also the Levites will be officials before you. Behave courageously, and the LORD will be with the good" (2 Chron. 19:11).

Principle: "Take courage as you fulfill your duties, and may the Lord be with those who do what is right" (NLT).

Prayer:
1. I receive grace to do what is right, in Jesus' name.
2. Fear contending against my success, be defeated, in Jesus' name.

Faith & Love

"He who fears God has nothing else to fear. We should stand in such awe of the living Lord that all the threats that can be used by the proudest persecutor should have no more effect upon us than the whistling of the wind."

—Charles H. Spurgeon

Day 185

It is written: "Then the LORD answered me and said: 'Write the vision and make it plain on tablets, that he may run who reads it. For the vision is yet for an appointed time; but at the end it will speak, and it will not lie. Though it tarries, wait for it; because it will surely come, it will not tarry'" (Hab. 2:2-3).

Principle: Recording your decisions against your fear hastens you toward the goal of success.

Prayer: 1. Every delayed blessing of mine be quickened unto manifestation, in Jesus' name.

2. I receive grace to patiently wait on God for miracles, in Jesus' name.

Day 186

It is written: "Behold the proud, his soul is not upright in him; but the just shall live by his faith" (Hab. 2:4).

Principle: The proud trust in themselves, but the just shall live by their faithfulness.

Prayer:
1. I pray my faith not to fail in spite of my trials, in Jesus' name.
2. I shall surely live by faith, in Jesus' name.

Day 187

It is written: "For the earth will be filled with the knowledge of the glory of the LORD, as the waters cover the sea" (Hab. 2:14).

Principle: Awareness of God's glory weakens your fears.

Prayer:
1. O Lord God, fill me with the knowledge of Your glory, in Jesus' name.
2. As the waters cover the sea, O Lord God, cover me with Your love and glory, in Jesus' name.

Day 188

It is written: "O LORD, I have heard Your speech and was afraid; O LORD, revive Your work in the midst of the years! In the midst of the years make it known; in wrath remember mercy" (Hab. 3:2).

Principle: God's power saves you from fear and His mercies turn away wrath.

Prayer:
1. O mercies of God, deliver me from wrath, in Jesus' name.
2. Thank You, Almighty God, for renewing Your mercies every day in my life, in Jesus' name.

Day 189

It is written: "Though the fig tree may not blossom, nor fruit be on the vines; though the labor of the olive may fail, and the fields yield no food; though the flock may be cut off from the fold, and there be no herd in the stalls—Yet I will rejoice in the LORD, I will joy in the God of my salvation. The LORD God is my strength; He will make my feet like deer's feet, and He will make me walk on my high hills" (Hab. 3:17-19).

Principle: Be as sure-footed as a deer over the mountains of fear.

Prayer: 1. "I will rejoice in the Lord, I will joy in the God of my salvation" (Hab. 3:18), in Jesus' name.

2. The Lord God is my strength; therefore, I overcome fear, in Jesus' name.

Day 190

It is written: "Now if God so clothes the grass of the field, which today is, and tomorrow is thrown into the oven, will He not much more clothe you, O you of little faith?" (Matt. 6:30).

Principle: However little your faith is, do not resign to fear.

Prayer:
1. By faith in Christ Jesus, I conquer my fears, in Jesus' name.
2. My life is too precious to let fear ruin it; therefore, I prevail over my fears, in Jesus' name.

Day 191

It is written: "And Jesus said to him, 'I will come and heal him.' The centurion answered and said, 'Lord, I am not worthy that You should come under my roof. But only speak a word, and my servant will be healed. For I also am a man under authority, having soldiers under me. And I say to this one, "Go," and he goes; and to another, "Come," and he comes; and to my servant, "Do this," and he does it'" (Matt. 8:7-10).

Principle: Fear is bound to submit to you when you're under the authority of God Almighty.

Prayer:
1. By the authority of God Almighty whom I submit to, I overcome fear, in Jesus' name.
2. Through the authority of the Word of God, I conquer my fears, in Jesus' name.

DAY 192

It is written: "But He said to them, "Why are you fearful, O you of little faith?" Then He arose and rebuked the winds and the sea, and there was a great calm" (Matt. 8:26).

Principle: Arise and rebuke your fear, and you shall be greatly calmed.

Prayer:
1. I rebuke the rage of fear set against me, in Jesus' name.
2. I decree great calmness upon my life, in Jesus' name.

DAY 193

It is written: "Then behold, they brought to Him a paralytic lying on a bed. When Jesus saw their faith, He said to the paralytic, 'Son, be of good cheer; your sins are forgiven you'" (Matt. 9:2).

Principle: Fear can be sinful, but assurance of forgiveness restores hope.

Prayer:
1. O Lord God, I ask that You forgive me of my sinful fear, in Jesus' name.
2. I'm of good cheer because my sins are forgiven, in Jesus' name.

Day 194

> **It is written:** "But Jesus turned around, and when He saw her He said, 'Be of good cheer, daughter; your faith has made you well.' And the woman was made well from that hour" (Matt. 9:22).
>
> **Principle:** Being cheerful in the midst of your fear is wellness to your soul.
>
> **Prayer:** 1. I'm encouraged, cheerful, and full of faith, in Jesus' name.
>
> 2. I receive wellness of soul, in Jesus' name.

Day 195

It is written: "Then He touched their eyes, saying, 'According to your faith let it be to you'" (Matt. 9:29).

Principle: A touch from God brings you out of fear—be open minded.

Prayer: 1. I have faith in God, so I overcome my fears, in Jesus' name.

2. O God, touch me so I can touch others, in Jesus' name.

Day 196

It is written: "And immediately Jesus stretched out His hand and caught him, and said to him, 'O you of little faith, why did you doubt?'" (Matt. 14:31).

Principle: God is always reaching out to you—be willing and open-minded.

Prayer:
1. I reach out to accept divine deliverance from fear, in Jesus' name.
2. Thank You, God, for reaching out to me in love, in Jesus' name.

Day 197

It is written: "Then Jesus answered and said to her, 'O woman, great is your faith! Let it be to you as you desire.' And her daughter was healed from that very hour" (Matt. 15:28).

Principle: Faith makes great requests granted, but fear doubts.

Prayer: 1. I receive faith to ask and receive without doubting, in Jesus' name.

2. Thank You, God, for granting my request, in Jesus' name.

Day 198

It is written: "But Jesus, being aware of it, said to them, 'O you of little faith, why do you reason among yourselves because you have brought no bread?'" (Matt. 16: 8).

Principle: Fear makes you worry about your lack, but faith in God rejoices over it.

Prayer:
1. I rejoice over my lack because it is already provided for, in Jesus' name.
2. Thank You, God, for providing all that I lack, in Jesus' name.

Day 199

It is written: "So Jesus said to them, 'Because of your unbelief; for assuredly, I say to you, if you have faith as a mustard seed, you will say to this mountain, "Move from here to there," and it will move; and nothing will be impossible for you'" (Matt. 17:20).

Principle: Faith moves your fear away without sensing impossibilities.

Prayer:
1. Good things shall not be impossible for me to inherit, in Jesus' name.
2. I claim victory over impossibilities for good things, in Jesus' name.

Day 200

It is written: "Woe to you, scribes and Pharisees, hypocrites! For you pay tithe of mint and anise and cummin, and have neglected the weightier matters of the law: justice and mercy and faith. These you ought to have done, without leaving the others undone" (Matt. 23:23).

Principle: Fear makes you neglect weightier matters and dwell on minor ones.

Prayer:
1. I receive grace to be sensitive both to minor and major issues of life, in Jesus' name.
2. Power to do it right, I receive, in Jesus' name.

Day 201

It is written: "When Jesus saw their faith, He said to the paralytic, 'Son, your sins are forgiven you'" (Mark 2:5).

Principle: Forgiving, and accepting forgiveness, gives you confidence over your fears.

Prayer: 1. Thank You, God Almighty, for forgiving all my sins, in Jesus' name.

2. Thank You, my Lord Jesus Christ, for paying the price of my forgiveness, in Jesus' name.

Day 202

It is written: "But He said to them, 'Why are you so fearful? How is it that you have no faith?'" (Mark 4:40).

Principle: Fearfulness and faithlessness are venom to your soul—refute them.

Prayer: 1. O Lord God, deliver me from fearfulness and faithlessness, in Jesus' name.

2. I'm not fearful, but full of faith and thanksgiving, in Jesus' name.

DAY 203

It is written: "And He said to her, 'Daughter, your faith has made you well. Go in peace, and be healed of your affliction'" (Mark 5:34).

Principle: Progressing in faith with peace is an antidote to fear.

Prayer:
1. I am healed of my afflictions, in Jesus' name.
2. I progress in faith with peace, in Jesus' name.

Day 204

It is written: "From there He arose and went to the region of Tyre and Sidon. And He entered a house and wanted no one to know it, but He could not be hidden" (Mark 7:24).

Principle: True faith in God cannot escape notice and will likely affect others.

Prayer: 1. I receive grace to positively affect others, in Jesus' name.

2. I refuse to be negatively affected, in Jesus' name.

Day 205

It is written: "Then Jesus said to him, 'Go your way; your faith has made you well.' And immediately he received his sight and followed Jesus on the road" (Mark 10:52).

Principle: Following Jesus Christ in every way makes you whole.

Prayer: 1. I have decided to follow Jesus Christ all the way, no turning back, in Jesus' name.

2. Thank You, my Lord Jesus Christ, for making me whole, in Jesus' name.

Day 206

It is written: "So Jesus answered and said to them, 'Have faith in God. For assuredly, I say to you, whoever says to this mountain, "Be removed and be cast into the sea," and does not doubt in his heart, but believes that those things he says will be done, he will have whatever he says. Therefore I say to you, whatever things you ask when you pray, believe that you receive them, and you will have them'" (Mark 11:22-24).

Principle: Faith in God breaks the yoke of fear.

Prayer:
1. My faith in God shall not fail, in Jesus' name.
2. I pray my faith in God will increase daily, in Jesus' name.

Day 207

It is written: "When He saw their faith, He said to him, 'Man, your sins are forgiven you'" (Luke 5:20).

Principle: Sins forgiven means mercies received.

Prayer: 1. Thank You, God, for Your lovingkindness in forgiving me for my sins, in Jesus' name.

2. I receive grace to live right, in Jesus' name.

Day 208

It is written: "But rise and stand on your feet; for I have appeared to you for this purpose, to make you a minister and a witness both of the things which you have seen and of the things which I will yet reveal to you. I will deliver you from the Jewish people, as well as from the Gentiles, to whom I now send you, to open their eyes, in order to turn them from darkness to light, and from the power of Satan to God, that they may receive forgiveness of sins and an inheritance among those who are sanctified by faith in Me" (Acts 26:16-18).

Principle: Defending your faith in God before people is confronting your fears.

Prayer:
1. Open my eyes, O Lord, to turn from darkness to light, in Jesus' name.
2. I receive grace to partake in the inheritance of the righteous, in Jesus' name.

Day 209

It is written: "That is, that I may be encouraged together with you by the mutual faith both of you and me" (Rom. 1:12).

Principle: Mutual encouragement fights our fears.

Prayer: 1. I receive grace to encourage those around me, in Jesus' name.

2. I shall not faint in encouraging myself and others, in Jesus' name.

Day 210

It is written: "For I am not ashamed of the gospel of Christ, for it is the power of God to salvation for everyone who believes, for the Jew first and also for the Greek. For in it the righteousness of God is revealed from faith to faith; as it is written, 'The just shall live by faith'" (Rom. 1:16-17).

Principle: Unashamed goodness is a fearless goodness.

Prayer:
1. I boldly declare that I am not ashamed of the gospel of Christ, in Jesus' name.
2. The power of Almighty God is at work in my life to save, heal, and deliver, in Jesus' name.

Day 211

It is written: "And not being weak in faith, he did not consider his own body, already dead (since he was about a hundred years old), and the deadness of Sarah's womb" (Rom. 4:19).

Principle: Faith considers not the impossibilities, but fear does.

Prayer:
1. I confess that I'm not weakened in faith but am growing strong daily, in Jesus' name.
2. I shall not stumble through faithlessness, in Jesus' name.

Day 212

It is written: "He did not waver at the promise of God through unbelief, but was strengthened in faith, giving glory to God" (Rom. 4:20).

Principle: Fear makes you waver, but faith makes you grow stronger.

Prayer:
1. I pray that I shall never waver in faith but will fix my eyes on God Almighty, in Jesus' name.
2. I shall grow strong in faith and in my walk with God, in Jesus' name.

Day 213

It is written: "Therefore, having been justified by faith, we have peace with God through our Lord Jesus Christ" (Rom. 5:1).

Principle: Faith triumphs over fear when you have the peace of reconciliation with God and others.

Prayer: 1. Blood of Jesus, reconcile me to peace, love, joy, and my fellow man, in Jesus' name.

2. I have been justified by faith so I can renounce fear, in Jesus' name.

Day 214

It is written: "Through whom also we have access by faith into this grace in which we stand, and rejoice in hope of the glory of God" (Rom. 5:2).

Principle: Fear gains access to our lives when we let it, but faith shut the doors against it.

Prayer:
1. I firmly and safely stand in my victory against fear, in Jesus' name.
2. I shut the door to fear and open the door to faith in my life, in Jesus' name.

Day 215

It is written: "But the righteousness of faith speaks in this way, 'Do not say in your heart, "Who will ascend into heaven?" (that is, to bring Christ down from above) or, "Who will descend into the abyss?" (that is, to bring Christ up from the dead). But what does it say? 'The word is near you, in your mouth and in your ear' (that is, the word of faith which we preach)" (Rom. 10:6-8).

Principle: When your efforts to overcome fear fail, a word of faith from the heart confirms your victory.

Prayer:
1. I decree through faith, that my efforts to overcome fear shall not fail, in Jesus' name.
2. Henceforth, right words shall proceed from my heart and mouth, in Jesus' name.

Day 216

It is written: "That if you confess with your mouth the Lord Jesus and believe in your heart that God has raised Him from the dead, you will be saved. For with the heart one believes unto righteousness, and with the mouth confession is made unto salvation" (Rom. 10:9-10).

Principle: Believing God from your heart and confessing with your mouth strengthen you against your fear.

Prayer:
1. Lord Jesus Christ, I believe You from my heart and I confess You as my Lord and Savior, in Jesus' name.
2. I believe I'm victorious over all my fears, in Jesus' name.

Day 217

It is written: "For the Scripture says, 'Whoever believes on Him will not be put to shame'" (Rom. 10:11).

Principle: Fear can be shameful, so shame your fears.

Prayer: 1. I believe in You, O God, therefore, I shall never be ashamed, in Jesus' name.

2. I shame my fears, in Jesus' name.

Day 218

It is written: "So then faith comes by hearing, and hearing by the word of God" (Rom. 10:17).

Principle: Hearing the Word of God is the only antidote to fear.

Prayer: 1. O God, give me a hearing ear and a receiving heart, in Jesus' name.

2. Let the Word of God bless my heart always, in Jesus' name.

Day 219

It is written: "Because of unbelief they were broken off, and you stand by faith. Do not be haughty, but fear. For if God did not spare the natural branches, He may not spare you either" (Rom. 11:20-21).

Principle: Being high-minded and arrogant reveals your secret fears.

Prayer: 1. May every secret fear of mine be purged by the blood of Jesus, in Jesus' name.

2. I repent of my high-mindedness and arrogance, in Jesus' name.

Day 220

It is written: "I beseech you therefore, brethren, by the mercies of God, that you present your bodies a living sacrifice, holy, acceptable to God, which is your reasonable service" (Rom. 12:1).

Principle: Decisive dedication and devotion to God establish you above fear.

Prayer:
1. I make a decisive and dedicated decision to worship God Almighty through my Lord Jesus Christ, in Jesus' name.
2. I present myself as a living sacrifice, holy and acceptable unto God, in Jesus' name.

DAY 221

It is written: "And do not be conformed to this world, but be transformed by the renewing of your mind, that you may prove what is that good and acceptable and perfect will of God" (Rom. 12:2).

Principle: Overcoming fear is all about change, new ideals, and attitude.

Prayer: 1. I am transformed by the renewing of my mind, in Jesus' name.

2. I will not conform to the world but will be fashioned after righteousness, in Jesus' name.

Day 222

It is written: "For I say, through the grace given to me, to everyone who is among you, not to think of himself more highly than he ought to think, but to think soberly, as God has dealt to each one a measure of faith" (Rom. 12:3).

Principle: Having an exaggerated opinion of myself increases my fear, but rating my ability with sober judgment brings me out of fear.

Prayer: 1. I receive grace to be honest with myself in all things, in Jesus' name.

2. I refute a wrong measure of my value, but I will value myself according to God's standard, in Jesus' name.

Day 223

It is written: "Having then gifts differing according to the grace that is given to us, let us use them: if prophecy, let us prophesy in proportion to our faith; or ministry, let us use it in our ministering; he who teaches, in teaching; he who exhorts, in exhortation; he who gives, with liberality; he who leads, with diligence; he who shows mercy, with cheerfulness" (Rom. 12:6-8).

Principle: Expressing myself with simplicity, liberality, and singleness of mind with genuine cheerfulness makes me forget my fears.

Prayer:
1. Thank God for giving me the ability to do things very well, in Jesus' name.
2. According to my portion of faith, I overcome my fears, in Jesus' name.

Day 224

It is written: "Let love be without hypocrisy. Abhor what is evil. Cling to what is good" (Rom. 12:9).

Principle: Expressing and receiving sincere, real love will quench your fear.

Prayer: 1. I shall stand upright for good all my life, in Jesus' name.

2. Evil shall not cling unto me, in Jesus' name.

Day 225

It is written: "Be kindly affectionate to one another with brotherly love, in honor giving preference to one another" (Rom. 12:10).

Principle: "Love each other with genuine affection, and take delight in honoring each other" (NLT).

Prayer: 1. I take delight in honoring God and others, in Jesus' name.

2. O Lord God, give me genuine affection, in Jesus' name.

Day 226

It is written: "Not lagging in diligence, fervent in spirit, serving the Lord" (Rom. 12:11).

Principle: Not lagging behind in diligence, but enthusiastically progressing in good works makes you a success.

Prayer:
1. I shun laziness in pursing my life's goal, in Jesus' name.
2. I shall be diligent in every good work, in Jesus' name.

Day 227

It is written: "Rejoicing in hope, patient in tribulation, continuing steadfastly in prayer" (Rom. 12:12).

Principle: "Be glad for all God is planning for you. Be patient in trouble, and always be prayerful" (NLT).

Prayer:
1. I'm steadfast and patient in believing God for unceasing blessings, in Jesus' name.
2. I'm glad for all God is planning for me, in Jesus' name.

Day 228

> **It is written:** "Repay no one evil for evil. Have regard for good things in the sight of all men" (Rom. 12:17).
>
> **Principle:** Respect what is right, take thought for others, and watch fear of men disappearing.
>
> **Prayer:** 1. Thank You, Lord God, for giving me victory over the fear of men, in Jesus' name.
>
> 2. I'll respect what is right and shun evil, in Jesus' name.

Day 229

It is written: "If it is possible, as much as depends on you, live peaceably with all men" (Rom. 12:18).

Principle: Living in peace with myself and other dispels my fears.

Prayer:
1. My Lord Jesus Christ, the Prince of peace, reigns in my life, in Jesus' name.
2. I receive grace to live peaceably with myself and everyone, in Jesus' name.

Day 230

It is written: "Do not be overcome by evil, but overcome evil with good" (Rom. 12:21).

Principle: "Don't let evil get the best of you, but conquer evil by doing good" (NLT).

Prayer: 1. Evil shall not get any part of me, but righteousness shall have all of me, in Jesus' name.

2. I conquer evil by doing good, in Jesus' name.

Day 231

It is written: "Receive one who is weak in the faith, but not to disputes over doubtful things" (Rom. 14:1).

Principle: Apply wisdom when people argue and dispute with your opinions—never give in to fear.

Prayer: 1. I humbly receive godly direction over every criticism, in Jesus' name.

2. I subdue every criticism against my life to the lordship of Jesus, in Jesus' name.

DAY 232

It is written: "Do you have faith? Have it to yourself before God. Happy is he who does not condemn himself in what he approves" (Rom. 14:22).

Principle: " ... Blessed are those who do not condemn themselves by doing something they know it all right" (NLT).

Prayer:
1. I refute every condemnation that brings fear into my life, in Jesus' name.
2. I shall without fear do what is right and good in the sight of God Almighty, in Jesus' name.

Day 233

It is written: "But he who doubts is condemned if he eats, because he does not eat from faith; for whatever is not from faith is sin" (Rom. 14:23).

Principle: "Whatever is done without a conviction of its approval by God is sinful." (Amplified Bible).

Prayer:
1. I receive divine approval as authority over all my undertakings, in Jesus' name.
2. I reject anything not approved by God Almighty in my life, in Jesus' name.

Day 234

It is written: "That your faith should not be in the wisdom of men but in the power of God" (1 Cor. 2:5).

Principle: However good human wisdom may be, it is limited, but trusting the unlimited power of God provides wisdom to overcome fear.

Prayer: 1. O Lord God, I put my trust in Your unlimited power and wisdom to overcome my fears, in Jesus' name.

2. O God, empower me with Your wisdom to overcome my fears, in Jesus' name.

Day 235

It is written: "Though I speak with the tongues of men and of angels, but have not love, I have become sounding brass or a clanging cymbal. And though I have the gift of prophecy, and understand all mysteries and all knowledge, and though I have all faith, so that I could remove mountains, but have not love, I am nothing. And though I bestow all my goods to feed the poor, and though I give my body to be burned, but have not love, it profits me nothing. Love suffers long and is kind; love does not envy; love does not parade itself, is not puffed up" (1 Cor. 13:1-4).

Principle: Expressing love through patience and kindness is a practical way to overcome your fears.

Prayer:
1. O Lord, grant me grace to always put my love into action, in Jesus' name.
2. I receive grace to be patient and kind in overcoming my fears, in Jesus' name.

Day 236

It is written: "[Love] … does not behave rudely, does not seek its own, is not provoked, thinks no evil" (1 Cor. 13:5).

Principle: Even though I'm fearful, politeness and courtesy are sure ways of expressing my love in society.

Prayer:
1. I overcome rudeness and discourteous attitudes, in Jesus' name.
2. I shall not behave myself unseemingly, in Jesus' name.

DAY 237

It is written: "[Love] ... does not behave rudely, does not seek its own, is not provoked, thinks no evil" (1 Cor. 13:5).

Principle: Fear may get you irritated, bitter, and resentful, but a good temper is love revealed in your disposition.

Prayer:
1. O Lord God, heal me of bitterness and irritation, in Jesus' name.
2. I receive grace to seek only the good of others, in Jesus' name.

Day 238

It is written: "[Love] ... does not rejoice in iniquity, but rejoices in the truth" (1 Cor. 13:6).

Principle: Being made glad by the goodness of others graciously permits you to see your own goodness.

Prayer:
1. I shall always rejoice in the goodness of others, in Jesus' name.
2. Let my goodness be no longer hidden but be made manifest, in Jesus' name.

Day 239

> **It is written:** "[Love] ... bears all things, believes all things, hopes all things, endures all things" (1 Cor. 13:7).
>
> **Principle:** Be ready to believe the best of every person and your hope will be unfading under any circumstance.
>
> **Prayer:** 1. I can graciously endure any circumstance without weakening, and I can be victorious, in Jesus' name.
>
> 2. My hope for victory over fear shall not fade away, in Jesus' name.

Day 240

It is written: "Love never fails. But whether there are prophecies, they will fail; whether there are tongues, they will cease; whether there is knowledge, it will vanish away" (1 Cor. 13:8).

Principle: Love never fades out or become obsolete in the face of fear.

Prayer:
1. Because God is love, my love for God and people shall not become obsolete, in Jesus' name.
2. I shall not fail in love, in Jesus' name.

Day 241

It is written: "And now abide faith, hope, love, these three; but the greatest of these is love" (1 Cor. 13:13).

Principle: With confident expectation and true affection for God and man, fear is conquered.

Prayer: 1. I shall not fail in faith, hope, and love, in Jesus' name.

2. I shall always abound in faith, hope, and love, in Jesus' name.

Day 242

It is written: "And if Christ is not risen, then our preaching is empty and your faith is also empty" (1 Cor. 15:14).

Principle: It is a vain pursuit to try to overcome fear without resurrection power.

Prayer:
1. I shall not engage in an empty and fruitless fight against fear, in Jesus' name.
2. Resurrection power of my Lord and Saviour Jesus Christ, quicken me out of my fear, in Jesus' name.

Day 243

It is written: "And if Christ is not risen, your faith is futile; you are still in your sins!" (1 Cor. 15:17).

Principle: Faith becomes futile and delusional when fear controls—therefore, put fear under control.

Prayer:
1. I break the control of fear over my life, in Jesus' name.
2. My faith against fear shall ever be alive and not dead, in Jesus' name.

Day 244

It is written: "Watch, stand fast in the faith, be brave, be strong" (1 Cor. 16:13).

Principle: Be alert and on your guard. Stand true to what you believe and fear shall be defeated.

Prayer: 1. I am watchful, brave, and strong against fear, in Jesus' name.

2. Fear shall no longer break my defenses, in Jesus' name.

DAY 245

It is written: "Let all that you do be done with love" (1 Cor. 16:14).

Principle: "Let everything you do be done in love (true love to God and man as inspired by God's love for us)" (Amplified Bible).

Prayer: 1. I pray that God's love will inspire true love in me, in Jesus' name.

2. I shall, through the grace of God, do all things in love, in Jesus' name.

Day 246

It is written: "Not that we have dominion over your faith, but are fellow workers for your joy; for by faith you stand" (2 Cor. 1:24).

Principle: Mutual agreement to work together in overcoming fear easily breaks the yoke.

Prayer:
1. O Lord God, connect me with the people who will work together with me to overcome my fears, in Jesus' name.
2. I overcome all disunity and lack of cooperation, in Jesus' name.

Day 247

It is written: "And since we have the same spirit of faith, according to what is written, 'I believed and therefore I spoke,' we also believe and therefore speak" (2 Cor. 4:13).

Principle: Believing in your heart that you can overcome fear, and regularly confessing it, puts fear under your feet.

Prayer: 1. I believe, and therefore, I will speak against my fear so that it will be defeated, in Jesus' name.

2. I put my fear under my feet, in Jesus' name.

Day 248

It is written: "For we walk by faith, not by sight" (2 Cor. 5:7).

Principle: Regulating and conducting yourself through faith and not by circumstances around you confirms your victory over fear.

Prayer: 1. O God, teach me to walk by faith and not by sight, in Jesus' name.

2. I shall judge rightly and not just by appearances alone, in Jesus' name.

DAY 249

It is written: "Therefore, if anyone is in Christ, he is a new creation; old things have passed away; behold, all things have become new" (2 Cor. 5:17).

Principle: You can't be the same anymore when fear is defeated in your life; a new life springs up.

Prayer:
1. I am a new creature in Christ Jesus. The old is gone but the new joyful life has come, in Jesus' name.
2. Henceforth, I behold the benefits of new life, in Jesus' name.

DAY 250

It is written: "Now all things are of God, who has reconciled us to Himself through Jesus Christ, and has given us the ministry of reconciliation" (2 Cor. 5:18).

Principle: When fear is no longer fearful to you, bring others out of fear through your words and deeds.

Prayer:
1. O God, help me to reconcile others to peace, in Jesus' name.
2. I shall live to bring others into harmony with God, in Jesus' name.

Day 251

It is written: "That is, that God was in Christ reconciling the world to Himself, not imputing their trespasses to them, and has committed to us the word of reconciliation" (2 Cor. 5:19).

Principle: When you no longer fear your fears, tell others; it's a wonderful message.

Prayer: 1. Thank You, God, for committing unto me the message of reconciliation, in Jesus' name.

2. I shall, through the grace of God, reconcile others to peace, in Jesus' name.

Day 252

It is written: "Now then, we are ambassadors for Christ, as though God were pleading through us: we implore you on Christ's behalf, be reconciled to God" (2 Cor. 5:20).

Principle: The reconciled are ambassadors for Christ in order to reconcile others.

Prayer:
1. I shall live to fulfill my role as an ambassador for Christ, in Jesus' name.
2. The message of reconciliation shall not cease from being in my mouth, in Jesus' name.

Day 253

It is written: "For He made Him who knew no sin to be sin for us, that we might become the righteousness of God in Him" (2 Cor. 5:21).

Principle: It took a sacrificial offering from God to reconcile us to Him—cherish it and accept it.

Prayer:
1. I shall ever live to cherish the eternal sacrificial offering God made for my sake, in Jesus' name.
2. The reconciling grace of God in my life shall not be in vain, in Jesus' name.

DAY 254

It is written: "Do not be unequally yoked together with unbelievers. For what fellowship has righteousness with lawlessness? And what communion has light with darkness? And what accord has Christ with Belial? Or what part has a believer with an unbeliever? And what agreement has the temple of God with idols? For you are the temple of the living God. As God has said: 'I will dwell in them and walk among them. I will be their God, and they shall be My people.' Therefore, 'Come out from among them and be separate,' says the Lord. 'Do not touch what is unclean, and I will receive you. I will be a Father to you, and you shall be My sons and daughters,' says the LORD Almighty" (2 Cor. 6:14-18).

Principle: Do not make a mismatched alliance with fear—sever yourself from it.

Prayer:
1. My life is separated from fear and its bondages, in Jesus' name.
2. I sever myself from every unholy alliance with fear, in Jesus' name.

Day 255

It is written: "Therefore, having these promises, beloved, let us cleanse ourselves from all filthiness of the flesh and spirit, perfecting holiness in the fear of God" (2 Cor. 7:1).

Principle: Reverential fear of God brings your freedom from fear to completion.

Prayer:
1. O God, cleanse me from the filthiness of fear, in Jesus' name.
2. Henceforth, fear shall no longer defile my life, in Jesus' name.

Day 256

It is written: "For godly sorrow produces repentance leading to salvation, not to be regretted; but the sorrow of the world produces death. For observe this very thing, that you sorrowed in a godly manner: What diligence it produced in you, what clearing of yourselves, what indignation, what fear, what vehement desire, what zeal, what vindication! In all things you proved yourselves to be clear in this matter" (2 Cor. 7:10-11).

Principle: "For God can use sorrow in our lives to help us turn away from sin and seek salvation… ." (NLT).

Prayer:
1. I reject every ungodly sorrow in my life, in Jesus' name.
2. O God, let every grief in my life lead me into repentance, in Jesus' name.

Day 257

It is written: "Therefore I rejoice that I have confidence in you in everything" (2 Cor. 7:16).

Principle: Complete confidence and joy over fear is a certain victory.

Prayer:
1. Thank You, God Almighty, for making me happy always, in Jesus' name.
2. I receive grace to be happy in God always, in Jesus' name.

Day 258

It is written: "But as you abound in everything—in faith, in speech, in knowledge, in all diligence, and in your love for us—see that you abound in this grace also" (2 Cor. 8:7).

Principle: See to it that you excel in all your life's pursuits as you give from your heart—don't let fear hold you back.

Prayer:
1. I shall excel in all life's pursuits, in Jesus' name.
2. I shall not be lagging behind in giving to the needy, in Jesus' name.

Day 259

It is written: "Who comforts us in all our tribulation, that we may be able to comfort those who are in any trouble, with the comfort with which we ourselves are comforted by God" (2 Cor. 1:4).

Principle: Only God can truly console, comfort and encourage us when troubled by fear that we may help others.

Prayer:
1. Holy Spirit of the Living God, console, comfort and encourage me, in Jesus' name.
2. O God, help me to console, comfort and encourage those that are troubled with fear in Jesus' name.

Day 260

It is written: "For all the promises of God in Him are Yes, and in Him Amen, to the glory of God through us" (2 Cor. 1:20).

Principle: It is often said, "Jesus is the answer." This is absolutely true because the promises of God all find their answers in Him.

Prayer: 1. Thank You, my Lord Jesus, for dwelling in me to fulfill God's promises, in Jesus' name.

2. I say Amen in agreement to God's plan and purposes for my life, in Jesus' name.

DAY 261

It is written: "Lest Satan should take advantage of us; for we are not ignorant of his devices" (2 Cor. 2:11).

Principle: Fear may let Satan get advantage over you, more so, if you're ignorant of his wiles and intentions.

Prayer: 1. Blood of Jesus, abolish every evil intention and device against my life, in Jesus' name.

2. Henceforth, Satan shall not be able to take advantage of me, in Jesus' name.

Day 262

It is written: "Now thanks be to God who always leads us in triumph in Christ, and through us diffuses the fragrance of His knowledge in every place" (2 Cor. 2:14).

Principle: Join the chariots and engage in a triumphal procession over fear. Others have overcome; you can also.

Prayer:
1. I join in the joyful, triumphant procession over my fears, in Jesus' name.
2. I break asunder the triumph of fear over my life, in Jesus' name.

Day 263

It is written: "Not that we are sufficient of ourselves to think of anything as being from ourselves, but our sufficiency is from God" (2 Cor. 3:5).

Principle: You may consider yourself unfit and not qualified in your ability to overcome your fears, but trusting God makes you adequate to enjoy the victory.

Prayer:
1. Thank You, my Lord Jesus Christ, for making me fit to overcome my fears, in Jesus' name.
2. I conquer every sense of inadequacy and insufficiency through the blood of Jesus, in Jesus' name.

Day 264

It is written: "Now the Lord is the Spirit; and where the Spirit of the Lord is, there is liberty" (2 Cor. 3:17).

Principle: True freedom from fear comes when endued with the power of the Holy Spirit.

Prayer:
1. Thank You, my Lord God, for filling me with the Holy Spirit and power, in Jesus' name.
2. Henceforth, I walk in the liberty of the Holy Spirit and not in fear, in Jesus' name.

Day 265

It is written: "But we all, with unveiled face, beholding as in a mirror the glory of the Lord, are being transformed into the same image from glory to glory, just as by the Spirit of the Lord" (2 Cor. 3:18).

Principle: When you allow the Spirit of God to work within you, you can be a mirror that brightly reflects the glory of God.

Prayer:
1. Holy Spirit of the living God, work within me to reflect Your glory, in Jesus' name.
2. I shall reflect God's glory more and more every day, in Jesus' name.

Day 266

It is written: "Therefore, since we have this ministry, as we have received mercy, we do not lose heart. But we have renounced the hidden things of shame, not walking in craftiness nor handling the Word of God deceitfully, but by manifestation of the truth commending ourselves to every man's conscience in the sight of God" (2 Cor. 4:1-2).

Principle: Those who hide their disgraceful ways and secret thoughts, feelings, and desires are despondent with fear.

Prayer: 1. God, help me operate with a clear conscience before You and men, in Jesus' name.

2. I shall be truthful in all my doings, in Jesus' name.

Day 267

It is written: "For it is the God who commanded light to shine out of darkness, who has shone in our hearts to give the light of the knowledge of the glory of God in the face of Jesus Christ" (2 Cor. 4:6).

Principle: The light of God's knowledge can shine from your heart to illuminate your path from the darkness of fear.

Prayer:
1. O God, illuminate my path with the knowledge of Your majesty and glory, in Jesus' name.
2. O God, deliver me from the darkness of fear, in Jesus' name.

Day 268

It is written: "But we have this treasure in earthen vessels, that the excellence of the power may be of God and not of us" (2 Cor. 4:7).

Principle: As frail as human life is, we still possess a precious treasure, that God alone may take all the glory.

Prayer:
1. May every glorious treasure in me manifest itself to the glory of God, in Jesus' name.
2. O God, You deserve all the glory; therefore, take all the glory of my life, in Jesus' name.

Day 269

It is written: "We are hard-pressed on every side, yet not crushed; we are perplexed, but not in despair; persecuted, but not forsaken; struck down, but not destroyed—always carrying about in the body the dying of the Lord Jesus, that the life of Jesus also may be manifested in our body" (2 Cor. 4:8-10).

Principle: "We are pressed on every side by troubles, but we are not crushed and broken. We are perplexed, but we don't give up and quit. We are hunted down, but God never abandons us. We get knocked down, But we get up again and keep going" (v. 8-9, NLT).

Prayer:
1. Thank You, God Almighty, for safety over troubles, in Jesus' name.
2. In any way I've been hunted and knocked down, O Lord God, lift me up, in Jesus' name.

Day 270

It is written: "Therefore we do not lose heart. Even though our outward man is perishing, yet the inward man is being renewed day by day" (2 Cor. 4:16).

Principle: You may seem to be wasting away through fear, but your strength can be progressively renewed through Christ Jesus.

Prayer:
1. I decree that my life shall not be a waste, in Jesus' name.
2. O God, deliver me from wastage and renew my life with Your glory, in Jesus' name.

Day 271

It is written: "For our light affliction, which is but for a moment, is working for us a far more exceeding and eternal weight of glory" (2 Cor. 4:17).

Principle: Your present troubles cannot be compared with the immeasurable eternal glory yet to be revealed; therefore, endure and overcome.

Prayer:
1. O God, make me never lose focus on the eternal glory, in Jesus' name.
2. I will not lose heart; I will not give up in my pursuit for eternal glory, in Jesus' name.

Day 272

It is written: "While we do not look at the things which are seen, but at the things which are not seen. For the things which are seen are temporary, but the things which are not seen are eternal" (2 Cor. 4:18).

Principle: No trouble can outlast you; troubles are temporal, but you are of eternal worth and value.

Prayer:
1. O God, do not let momentary things make me lose my focus on You, in Jesus' name.
2. I fix my eyes on eternal glory and shall never miss it, in Jesus' name.

Day 273

It is written: "For we know that if our earthly house, this tent, is destroyed, we have a building from God, a house not made with hands, eternal in the heavens. For in this we groan, earnestly desiring to be clothed with our habitation which is from heaven, if indeed, having been clothed, we shall not be found naked. For we who are in this tent groan, being burdened, not because we want to be unclothed, but further clothed, that mortality may be swallowed up by life. Now He who has prepared us for this very thing is God, who also has given us the Spirit as a guarantee" (2 Cor. 5:1-5).

Principle: Why are you sighing, groaning, weighed down, depressed, and oppressed by fear? Shake it off and be clothed with joy and thanksgiving.

Prayer:
1. I refuse to groan, be weighed down, depressed, and oppressed by fear, in Jesus' name.
2. I arise out of every depressive and oppressive fear, in Jesus' name.

DAY 274

It is written: "So that you come short in no gift, eagerly waiting for the revelation of our Lord Jesus Christ, who will also confirm you to the end, that you may be blameless in the day of our Lord Jesus Christ" (1 Cor. 1:7-8).

Principle: Only God can establish you to the end, keep you steadfast, give you strength, and guarantee your vindication from fear.

Prayer:
1. I overcome accusation and indictment, in Jesus' name.
2. I will be irreproachable, in Jesus' name.

DAY 275

It is written: "For you see your calling, brethren, that not many wise according to the flesh, not many mighty, not many noble, are called. But God has chosen the foolish things of the world to put to shame the wise, and God has chosen the weak things of the world to put to shame the things which are mighty; and the base things of the world and the things which are despised God has chosen, and the things which are not, to bring to nothing the things that are, that no flesh should glory in His presence" (1 Cor. 1:26-29).

Principle: In overcoming fear, you need not be influential and powerful; neither of high and noble birth; nor low born and insignificant—refuse to be branded and treated with contempt.

Prayer: 1. I refuse to be branded and treated with contempt, in Jesus' name.

2. I shall only make my boast in the greatness of God Almighty, in Jesus' name.

Day 276

It is written: "For I determined not to know anything among you except Jesus Christ and Him crucified" (1 Cor. 2:2).

Principle: In all your knowings and acquaintances, resolve to magnify Jesus Christ as Lord and King and you will be fearless against your fear.

Prayer: 1. I am determined never to be enslaved by fear, in Jesus' name.

2. I am fearless against my fear, in Jesus' name.

Day 277

It is written: "But as it is written: 'Eye has not seen, nor ear heard, Nor have entered into the heart of man the things which God has prepared for those who love Him.' But God has revealed them to us through His Spirit. For the Spirit searches all things, yes, the deep things of God. For what man knows the things of a man except the spirit of the man which is in him? Even so no one knows the things of God except the Spirit of God. Now we have received, not the spirit of the world, but the Spirit who is from God, that we might know the things that have been freely given to us by God" (1 Cor. 2:9-12).

Principle: When you are fearless against your fear, you will regularly experience glorious things, which eye has not seen and ear has not heard.

Prayer:
1. Thank You, Lord God, for bringing to pass glorious things, which eyes have not seen nor ears heard, in my life, in Jesus' name.
2. O God, reveal unto me by Your Holy Spirit deep and glorious things, in Jesus' name.

Day 278

It is written: "These things we also speak, not in words which man's wisdom teaches but which the Holy Spirit teaches, comparing spiritual things with spiritual. But the natural man does not receive the things of the Spirit of God, for they are foolishness to him; nor can he know them, because they are spiritually discerned" (1 Cor. 2:13-14).

Principle: If the things of God are meaningless nonsense to you and you fail to recognize and become acquainted with Him, your struggle with fear will be eternal.

Prayer: 1. O God, make me know You progressively and always appreciate You, in Jesus' name.

2. Holy Spirit, reveal the fullness of God to me, in Jesus' name.

Day 279

It is written: "For no other foundation can anyone lay than that which is laid, which is Jesus Christ" (1 Cor. 3:11).

Principle: Shake fear off you from the foundation; it must not be rebuilt.

Prayer:
1. Jesus Christ is my sure foundation; therefore, my destiny is gloriously secured, in Jesus' name.
2. Any foundation contrary to the lordship of Jesus Christ in my life will crumble, in Jesus' name.

Day 280

It is written: "Do you not know that you are the temple of God and that the Spirit of God dwells in you? If anyone defiles the temple of God, God will destroy him. For the temple of God is holy, which temple you are" (1 Cor. 3:16-17).

Principle: Holy Spirit, your true Comforter, wants to be at home with you—will you allow Him to be?

Prayer:
1. Precious Holy Spirit, make Your permanent dwelling with me, in Jesus' name.
2. I open up my life to graciously accept the dwelling of the Holy Spirit, in Jesus' name.

Day 281

It is written: "For the wisdom of this world is foolishness with God. For it is written, 'He catches the wise in their own craftiness;' and again, 'The LORD knows the thoughts of the wise, that they are futile.' Therefore let no one boast in men. For all things are yours" (1 Cor. 3:19-21).

Principle: How futile the thoughts and reasonings of human wisdom to overcome fear—rely on God.

Prayer: 1. O God Almighty, I absolutely depend on You in overcoming fear. Help me, in Jesus' name.

2. O God, endue me with wisdom to overcome fear, in Jesus' name.

Day 282

It is written: "Moreover it is required in stewards that one be found faithful" (1 Cor. 4:2).

Principle: Leaders are stewards and should be faithful and without fear to serve the people.

Prayer: 1. O God, make me without fear and with faithfulness of heart, so I can love and serve Your people, in Jesus' name.

2. I am a faithful steward for God and His people, in Jesus' name.

DAY 283

It is written: "For who makes you differ from another? And what do you have that you did not receive? Now if you did indeed receive it, why do you boast as if you had not received it?" (1 Cor. 4:7).

Principle: "What makes you better than anyone else? What do you have that God hasn't given you? And if all you have is from God, why boast as though you have accomplished something on your own?" (NLT).

Prayer:
1. All that I have is given by God; therefore, I give Him thanks, in Jesus' name.
2. With God on my side, I accomplish every good thing in life, in Jesus' name.

Day 284

It is written: "You were bought at a price; do not become slaves of men. Brethren, let each one remain with God in that state in which he was called" (1 Cor. 7:23-24).

Principle: "God purchased you at a high price. Don't be enslaved by the world" (v. 23, NLT).

Prayer: 1. Thank You, Almighty God, for the eternal high price with which You purchased my life to ransom me, in Jesus' name.

2. I shall ever live for God and for His glory, in Jesus' name.

Day 285

It is written: "Do you not know that those who run in a race all run, but one receives the prize? Run in such a way that you may obtain it. And everyone who competes for the prize is temperate in all things. Now they do it to obtain a perishable crown, but we for an imperishable crown. Therefore I run thus: not with uncertainty. Thus I fight: not as one who beats the air. But I discipline my body and bring it into subjection, lest, when I have preached to others, I myself should become disqualified" (1 Cor. 9:24-27).

Principle: Are you a counterfeit? Examine yourself.

Prayer:
1. In the test and trial of life, I shall not be unfit, in Jesus' name.
2. I receive grace to discipline myself so as to gain divine approval, in Jesus' name.

Day 286

It is written: "Now all these things happened to them as examples, and they were written for our admonition, upon whom the ends of the ages have come" (1 Cor. 10:11).

Principle: Be a living example. Be fit for right actions.

Prayer:
1. I receive grace to take the right action, in Jesus' name.
2. Holy Spirit, always instruct me against wrong action, in Jesus' name.

Day 287

It is written: "Therefore let him who thinks he stands take heed lest he fall" (1 Cor. 10:12).

Principle: Stand firm against your fear with a steadfast mind.

Prayer:
1. Through the grace of God, I shall stand firm and steadfast, in Jesus' name.
2. O Lord God, uphold me from falling, in Jesus' name.

Day 288

It is written: "No temptation has overtaken you except such as is common to man; but God is faithful, who will not allow you to be tempted beyond what you are able, but with the temptation will also make the way of escape, that you may be able to bear it" (1 Cor. 10:13).

Principle: "God can be trusted not to let you be tempted and tried and assayed beyond your ability and strength of resistance and power to endure ... " (Amplified Bible).

Prayer:
1. Thank You, Almighty God, for making me escape fear traps, in Jesus' name.
2. Through the grace of God, I am capable, strong, and powerful to overcome fear, in Jesus' name.

Day 289

It is written: "Therefore, my beloved brethren, be steadfast, immovable, always abounding in the work of the Lord, knowing that your labor is not in vain in the Lord" (1 Cor. 15:58).

Principle: "For you know that nothing you do for the Lord is ever useless" (NLT).

Prayer: 1. I shall always abound in good work, in Jesus' name.

2. My labor in the Lord shall not be futile nor wasted, in Jesus' name.

Day 290

It is written: "Examine yourselves as to whether you are in the faith. Test yourselves. Do you not know yourselves, that Jesus Christ is in you?—unless indeed you are disqualified" (2 Cor. 13:5).

Principle: "Examine yourselves to see if your faith if really genuine … " (NLT).

Prayer: 1. Through the grace of God, I shall pass the tests and trials of life, in Jesus' name.

2. May every mark of disapproval in me be annulled, in Jesus Christ's name.

Day 291

It is written: "But they were hearing only, 'He who formerly persecuted us now preaches the faith which he once tried to destroy' And they glorified God in me" (Gal. 1:23-24).

Principle: True conversion turns you away from your fears and rage, which will be evident to all.

Prayer: 1. God Almighty is the author and the source of my life, worthy of honor and praise, in Jesus' name.

2. O God, let those who reviled me and are set out to ruin me, be divinely arrested, in Jesus Christ's name.

Day 292

It is written: "I have been crucified with Christ; it is no longer I who live, but Christ lives in me; and the life which I now live in the flesh I live by faith in the Son of God, who loved me and gave Himself for me" (Gal. 2:20).

Principle: Living for self is unprofitable, but living for God produces eternal reward.

Prayer: 1. I shall live for God and to His glory, in Jesus' name.

2. Thank You, my Lord Jesus Christ, for living in me and offering Yourself to me, in Jesus Christ's name.

Day 293

It is written: "I say then: Walk in the Spirit, and you shall not fulfill the lust of the flesh" (Gal. 5:16).

Principle: "But I say, walk and live habitually in the (Holy) Spirit responsive to and controlled and guided by the Spirit; then you will certainly not gratify the craving and desires of the flesh—of human nature without God" (Amplified Bible).

Prayer:
1. Henceforth, I shall be responsive to and controlled and guided by the Holy Spirit, in Jesus' name.
2. My cravings and desires shall be yielded to God, in Jesus' name.

Day 294

It is written: "Do not be deceived, God is not mocked; for whatever a man sows, that he will also reap. For he who sows to his flesh will of the flesh reap corruption, but he who sows to the Spirit will of the Spirit reap everlasting life" (Gal. 6:7-8).

Principle: The law of sowing and reaping operates in overcoming fear. You will surely harvest the consequences of your words and deeds.

Prayer:
1. O God, help me sow in righteousness and not in iniquity, in Jesus' name.
2. Holy Spirit, help me to sow rightly and harvest rightly, in Jesus' name.

Day 295

It is written: "And let us not grow weary while doing good, for in due season we shall reap if we do not lose heart" (Gal. 6:9).

Principle: In acting nobly and doing right, don't lose heart, never grow weary, faint not—you shall surely be rewarded.

Prayer:
1. In the name of Jesus, I shall not grow weary, neither shall I faint nor lose heart.
2. My glorious reward, manifest now, in Jesus' name.

Day 296

It is written: "Therefore, as we have opportunity, let us do good to all, especially to those who are of the household of faith" (Gal. 6:10).

Principle: You are a sure blessing to lots of people—they can't survive without you. When you fail, multitudes who are connected to you fail also, but when you succeed, pass it on.

Prayer:
1. O God, let me never miss out on any opportunity to bless others, in Jesus' name.
2. O God, bless me to bless others, in Jesus' name.

Day 297

It is written: "But God forbid that I should boast except in the cross of our Lord Jesus Christ, by whom the world has been crucified to me, and I to the world" (Gal. 6:14).

Principle: What interest determines your values and outlook on life?

Prayer:
1. O God, help me align my values in You and favor Your purpose for my life, in Jesus' name.
2. O God, let Your interest be my interest, and Your desire my desire, in Jesus' name.

Day 298

It is written: "From now on let no one trouble me, for I bear in my body the marks of the Lord Jesus" (Gal. 6:17).

Principle: Your wounds, scars, and hurts are brand marks and evidence of life's hurtful experiences.

Prayer:
1. Blood of Jesus, heal my wounds, scars, and hurts, in Jesus' name.
2. Holy Spirit, minister healing to my hurting heart, in Jesus' name.

Day 299

It is written: "Let no one despise your youth, but be an example to the believers in word, in conduct, in love, in spirit, in faith, in purity" (1 Tim. 4:12).

Principle: Celebrate your youthful life in love, faith, and purity; and reap a rewarding, fruitful life.

Prayer:
1. I consecrate my youthful life to God Almighty for profitable living, in Jesus' name.
2. Henceforth, I shall have a rewarding and fulfilling life, in Jesus' name.

Day 300

It is written: "Now godliness with contentment is great gain. For we brought nothing into this world, and it is certain we can carry nothing out" (1 Tim. 6:6-7).

Principle: "Contentment is a sense of inward sufficiency—it is great and abundant gain" (AMPLIFIED BIBLE).

Prayer:
1. I shall accompany my godliness with a deep sense of contentment, in Jesus' name.
2. O God, enable me to do my very best, to Your glory, in Jesus' name.

Day 301

It is written: "But those who desire to be rich fall into temptation and a snare, and into many foolish and harmful lusts which drown men in destruction and perdition. For the love of money is a root of all kinds of evil, for which some have strayed from the faith in their greediness, and pierced themselves through with many sorrows. But you, O man of God, flee these things and pursue righteousness, godliness, faith, love, patience, gentleness" (1 Tim. 6:9-11).

Principle: As good as money and wealth are, undue craving and pursuit of them may lead to a ruined end. Therefore, be diligent.

Prayer:
1. I re-establish my covenant to make wealth only as God would have me to do, in Jesus' name.
2. Thank You, Almighty God, for providing and meeting all my needs, to Your glory, in Jesus' name.

Day 302

It is written: "Fight the good fight of faith, lay hold on eternal life, to which you were also called and have confessed the good confession in the presence of many witnesses" (1 Tim. 6:12).

Principle: A fight of faith is a fight that is worth fighting with all your might, until destiny is achieved and life transformed.

Prayer:
1. O God, help me not to engage in wrong battles, in Jesus' name.
2. I shall not be defeated in the battle of life, in Jesus' name.

Day 303

It is written: "You therefore must endure hardship as a good soldier of Jesus Christ. No one engaged in warfare entangles himself with the affairs of this life, that he may please him who enlisted him as a soldier" (2 Tim. 2:3-4).

Principle: Hardship, endurance, and discipline are qualities of a good solider, which you are, unless you've resigned to defeat.

Prayer: 1. I break free from every entanglement hindering my purpose in life, in Jesus' name.

2. As a victorious soldier, I shall not live below my expectations, in Jesus' name.

Day 304

It is written: "Be diligent to present yourself approved to God, a worker who does not need to be ashamed, rightly dividing the word of truth" (2 Tim. 2:15).

Principle: Having been tested by trials, correctly analyze your life using the truth of God's Word.

Prayer:
1. O God, let the truth of Your Word correct my life, in Jesus' name.
2. I shall without shame handle the Word of God rightly, in Jesus' name.

Day 305

It is written: "But shun profane and idle babblings, for they will increase to more ungodliness" (2 Tim. 2:16).

Principle: Idle talk is unprofitable and vain; avoid it.

Prayer: 1. O God, I repent of all idle talk. Please forgive me, in Jesus' name.

2. My words and deeds shall be seasoned with salt to bless others, in Jesus' name.

Day 306

It is written: "Nevertheless the solid foundation of God stands, having this seal: 'The Lord knows those who are His,' and, 'Let everyone who names the name of Christ depart from iniquity'" (2 Tim. 2:19).

Principle: Build your life on the sure, firm, and unshaken foundation—Jesus Christ.

Prayer:
1. I reaffirm my faith and belief in Jesus Christ as my sure, firm, and unshaken foundation, in Jesus' name.
2. I renounce any other foundation besides my Lord and Savior, Jesus Christ, in Jesus' name.

Day 307

It is written: "All Scripture is given by inspiration of God, and is profitable for doctrine, for reproof, for correction, for instruction in righteousness, that the man of God may be complete, thoroughly equipped for every good work" (2 Tim. 3:16-17).

Principle: God's Word is divinely inspired to reproof, convict, correct, and discipline, which makes you proficient and fit for life.

Prayer:
1. I open my heart to You, O God, that Your Word may reproof, convict, and correct my ways, in Jesus' name.
2. Grace to obey Your Word, O God, I receive, in Jesus' name.

Day 308

It is written: "I have fought the good fight, I have finished the race, I have kept the faith" (2 Tim. 4:7).

Principle: Your struggle against fear is a worthy, honorable, and noble fight; keep firmly to faith till you put fear under your feet.

Prayer:
1. I shall keep firmly to the faith through the grace of God Almighty, in Jesus' name.
2. Grace to run well and finish well, I receive, in Jesus' name.

Day 309

It is written: "And the Lord will deliver me from every evil work and preserve me for His heavenly kingdom. To Him be glory forever and ever. Amen!" (2 Tim. 4:18).

Principle: You can be delivered and preserved from the assault of fear through the grace of God.

Prayer: 1. Thank You, God Almighty, for delivering and preserving my life from the assault of fear, in Jesus' name.

2. Every fear assault against my life, be quenched, in Jesus' name.

Day 310

It is written: "To the pure all things are pure, but to those who are defiled and unbelieving nothing is pure; but even their mind and conscience are defiled" (Titus 1:15).

Principle: Your state of mind determines your outlook and response to life, even your quality of life, so think rightly with undefiled conscience.

Prayer:
1. Holy Spirit's fire, purify my mind and conscience, in Jesus' name.
2. Holy Spirit, renew my inner man, in Jesus' name.

Day 311

It is written: "They profess to know God, but in works they deny Him, being abominable, disobedient, and disqualified for every good work" (Titus 1:16).

Principle: If what you do contradicts what you say, then you're disapproved by both God and men.

Prayer: 1. I consecrate my words and actions to God Almighty, that I might live a life worthy before God and men, in Jesus' name.

2. O Lord God, help me to align my words and actions with my belief in Christ, in Jesus' name.

Day 312

It is written: "For the grace of God that brings salvation has appeared to all men, teaching us that, denying ungodliness and worldly lusts, we should live soberly, righteously, and godly in the present age" (Titus 2:11-12).

Principle: God's grace makes us turn from godless living and sinful pleasures and live in self-control and right conduct.

Prayer:
1. I turn away from godless living and sinful pleasures, in Jesus' name.
2. I shall be temperate and upright in all my doings, in Jesus' name.

Day 313

It is written: "You do not become sluggish, but imitate those who through faith and patience inherit the promises" (Heb. 6:12).

Principle: Dullness and indifference are wrong approaches to overcoming fear, but absolute trust and confidence in God Almighty make you inherit the promises.

Prayer:
1. I break free from dullness and indifference to a fulfilling life in God Almighty, in Jesus' name.
2. O Lord God, I have absolute trust and confidence in You; please help me, in Jesus' name.

Day 314

It is written: "Therefore He is also able to save to the uttermost those who come to God through Him, since He always lives to make intercession for them" (Heb. 7:25).

Principle: Jesus Christ is forever interceding with God and intervening for us; trust Him and He will keep you to the end.

Prayer: 1. My Lord Jesus Christ, I love You and I'll trust You to the end, in Jesus' name.

2. Thank You, my Lord Jesus Christ, for making intercession on my behalf, in Jesus' name.

Day 315

It is written: "Let us draw near with a true heart in full assurance of faith, having our hearts sprinkled from an evil conscience and our bodies washed with pure water. Let us hold fast the confession of our hope without wavering, for He who promised is faithful" (Heb. 10:22-23).

Principle: Confronting your fears with an honest and sincere heart, without wavering, makes you a champion.

Prayer:
1. With full assurance of faith, I come before God Almighty, my Maker, through the blood of Jesus, in Jesus' name.
2. I confront my fears with an unwavering confidence through the blood of Jesus.

Day 316

It is written: "And let us consider one another in order to stir up love and good works" (Heb. 10:24).

Principle: Be fearless in encouraging others. Don't hold back in helpful deeds and noble activities.

Prayer: 1. O Lord God, I pour out my heart to love You and Your people; please help me, in Jesus' name.

2. I will not hold back from helpful deeds and noble activities, in Jesus' name.

Day 317

It is written: "Therefore do not cast away your confidence, which has great reward" (Heb. 10:35).

Principle: Fearless confidence in God Almighty yields glorious rewards.

Prayer: 1. I am fearlessly confident that God Almighty will help me to overcome my fears, in Jesus' name.

2. Thank You, O God, for gloriously rewarding me, in Jesus' name.

Day 318

It is written: "Now faith is the substance of things hoped for, the evidence of things not seen" (Heb. 11:1).

Principle: Faith is perceiving as real fact what is not revealed to the senses, the conviction of their reality.

Prayer:
1. My senses, be aligned with the conviction of unseen reality, in Jesus' name.
2. My unseen blessings, manifest now, in Jesus' name.

DAY 319

It is written: "For by it the elders obtained a good testimony" (Heb. 11:2).

Principle: A fearless, simple trust in God gains commendation before God and man.

Prayer:
1. My good testimony through faith, come to pass now, in Jesus' name.
2. My faith shall be strong always to uphold my testimonies, in Jesus' name.

Day 320

It is written: "But without faith it is impossible to please Him, for he who comes to God must believe that He is, and that He is a rewarder of those who diligently seek Him" (Heb. 11:6).

Principle: God is a faithful rewarder, sincerely seek Him and you'll be victorious over fear.

Prayer: 1. I shall not seek God in vain; I shall seek Him and find Him, in Jesus' name.

2. O God Almighty, the Holy One of Israel, I believe that You exist and that You're a great rewarder of Your people; bless me indeed, in Jesus' name.

Day 321

It is written: "For he waited for the city which has foundations, whose builder and maker is God" (Heb. 11:10).

Principle: Build your life on faith, not on fear, and you'll be fixed and firm for success.

Prayer:
1. Blood of Jesus, fix and make firm my foundation for success, in Jesus' name.
2. God is my Architect, Builder and Maker, in Jesus' name.

DAY 322

It is written: "And truly if they had called to mind that country from which they had come out, they would have had opportunity to return" (Heb. 11:15).

Principle: Whatever you've renounced as hindrances to success, don't be homesick for them.

Prayer: 1. I shall not lose focus on my divine heritage, in Jesus' name.

2. I shall not return to my vomit, in Jesus' name.

Day 323

It is written: "Choosing rather to suffer affliction with the people of God than to enjoy the passing pleasures of sin" (Heb. 11:25).

Principle: The pleasure of sin shall soon pass away; keep enduring in faith and righteousness.

Prayer: 1. I renounce the enticement of sin and iniquity in my life, in Jesus' name.

2. I shall always enjoy the divine presence, in Jesus' name.

Day 324

It is written: "Who through faith subdued kingdoms, worked righteousness, obtained promises, stopped the mouths of lions, quenched the violence of fire, escaped the edge of the sword, out of weakness were made strong, became valiant in battle, turned to flight the armies of the aliens" (Heb. 11:33-34).

Principle: Fear is a raging fire and a devouring sword—extinguish it.

Prayer:
1. Roaring lion of fear, you shall not prevail against me, in Jesus' name.
2. Raging fire of fear against my life, be quenched, in Jesus' name.

Day 325

It is written: "Therefore we also, since we are surrounded by so great a cloud of witnesses, let us lay aside every weight, and the sin which so easily ensnares us, and let us run with endurance the race that is set before us" (Heb. 12:1).

Principle: Fear can be an encumbrance and unnecessary weight that clings to and entangles us, so be actively persistent in confronting it.

Prayer:
1. I throw off the weight of fear holding me from progressing, in Jesus' name.
2. I decree there will be no more fear entanglement in my life, in Jesus' name.

Day 326

It is written: "Looking unto Jesus, the author and finisher of our faith, who for the joy that was set before Him endured the cross, despising the shame, and has sat down at the right hand of the throne of God" (Heb. 12:2).

Principle: Great joy lies before you as you cast off fear. Rely on Jesus to start and finish the good work.

Prayer:
1. My Lord Jesus Christ, You are the Source and Perfecter of my faith; help me indeed, in Jesus' name.
2. The good works in my life are perfected through the blood of Jesus, in Jesus' name.

Day 327

It is written: "You have not yet resisted to bloodshed, striving against sin" (Heb. 12:4).

Principle: Resist and withstand fear even with your last strength.

Prayer:
1. Thank You, my God, for empowering me against fear, in Jesus' name.
2. My strength shall not fail me in resisting fear, in Jesus' name.

Day 328

It is written: "Therefore, since we are receiving a kingdom which cannot be shaken, let us have grace, by which we may serve God acceptably with reverence and godly fear. For our God is a consuming fire" (Heb. 12:28-29).

Principle: A perpetual victory over fear involves offering to God pleasing service and acceptable worship.

Prayer:
1. I shall forever show gratitude to God Almighty for His goodness to me, in Jesus' name.
2. O Lord God, let my service and worship be acceptable and pleasing unto You, in Jesus' name.

Day 329

It is written: "Therefore by Him let us continually offer the sacrifice of praise to God, that is, the fruit of our lips, giving thanks to His name" (Heb. 13:15).

Principle: Engaging in praises constantly and at all times in spite of your fear confirms your supremacy over fear.

Prayer:
1. I thankfully acknowledge the awesome presence of God over my life with joy, in Jesus' name.
2. My soul magnifies the true and living God for victory over fear, in Jesus' name.

Day 330

It is written: "But do not forget to do good and to share, for with such sacrifices God is well pleased" (Heb. 13:16).

Principle: Be kind, be generous, help the needy, do it fearlessly.

Prayer:
1. I shall recognize and help the needy, in Jesus' name.
2. I shall, through the grace of God, offer well pleasing gifts to the needy, in Jesus' name.

Day 331

It is written: "My brethren, count it all joy when you fall into various trials, knowing that the testing of your faith produces patience. But let patience have its perfect work, that you may be perfect and complete, lacking nothing" (James 1:2-4).

Principle: "… whenever trouble comes your way, let it be an opportunity for joy" (NLT) (James 1:2).

Prayer:
1. I receive grace to overcome temptations and trials, in Jesus' name.
2. I quench every wave of temptation set against me, in Jesus' name.

Day 332

It is written: "If any of you lacks wisdom, let him ask of God, who gives to all liberally and without reproach, and it will be given to him. But let him ask in faith, with no doubting, for he who doubts is like a wave of the sea driven and tossed by the wind. For let not that man suppose that he will receive anything from the Lord; he is a double-minded man, unstable in all his ways" (James 1:5-8).

Principle: Double-mindedness makes you unstable and uncertain in your struggle with fear.

Prayer:
1. Blood of Jesus, heal me of double-mindedness, in Jesus' name.
2. Whatever I think, feel, or decide shall bring honor to the name of God Almighty, in Jesus' name.

Day 333

It is written: "Blessed is the man who endures temptation; for when he has been approved, he will receive the crown of life which the Lord has promised to those who love Him" (James 1:12).

Principle: Be patient under trial, because great reward awaits you.

Prayer:
1. I receive grace to endure temptations, in Jesus' name.
2. My glorious reward shall not elude me, in Jesus' name.

DAY 334

It is written: "Let no one say when he is tempted, 'I am tempted by God;' for God cannot be tempted by evil, nor does He Himself tempt anyone. But each one is tempted when he is drawn away by his own desires and enticed. Then, when desire has conceived, it gives birth to sin; and sin, when it is full-grown, brings forth death. Do not be deceived, my beloved brethren" (James 1:13-16).

Principle: "Evil desires lead to evil actions, and evil actions lead to death. So don't be misled … " (NLT).

Prayer:
1. O Lord God, transform my desires by Your Holy Spirit, in Jesus' name.
2. Through the blood of Jesus, I retrieve my steps from evil actions, in Jesus' name.

DAY 335

It is written: "Every good gift and every perfect gift is from above, and comes down from the Father of lights, with whom there is no variation or shadow of turning" (James 1:17).

Principle: Seeking for good things of life? Look up unto God Almighty, He gives the very best.

Prayer:
1. O Lord God, I ask that You bless me with good and perfect gifts, in Jesus' name.
2. Good and perfect gifts shall be my daily encounter, in Jesus' name.

Day 336

It is written: "So then, my beloved brethren, let every man be swift to hear, slow to speak, slow to wrath" (James 1:19).

Principle: Being a ready listener who is slow to take offense and watching your words are sure proof of a disciplined life.

Prayer:
1. I dedicate my hearing, speaking, and actions unto God Almighty, to minister life to everyone, in Jesus' name.
2. My words, hearing, and actions shall encourage and bless others, in Jesus' name.

Day 337

It is written: "For the wrath of man does not produce the righteousness of God" (James 1:20).

Principle: "Your anger can never make things right in God's sight" (NLT).

Prayer:
1. I repent of my anger, O God; forgive me, in Jesus' name.
2. I bind and cast the spirit of anger out of my life, in Jesus' name.

Day 338

It is written: "Therefore lay aside all filthiness and overflow of wickedness, and receive with meekness the implanted Word, which is able to save your souls" (James 1:21).

Principle: God's Word is strong enough to save your souls; humbly accept the message as you get rid of all uncleanness.

Prayer:
1. Thank You, God Almighty, for engrafting Your Word in my heart to save my soul, in Jesus' name.
2. I humbly accept the power of the Word of God to purge my life, in Jesus' name.

Day 339

It is written: "But be doers of the word, and not hearers only, deceiving yourselves. For if anyone is a hearer of the word and not a doer, he is like a man observing his natural face in a mirror; for he observes himself, goes away, and immediately forgets what kind of man he was. But he who looks into the perfect law of liberty and continues in it, and is not a forgetful hearer but a doer of the word, this one will be blessed in what he does" (James 1:22-25).

Principle: Great blessings await listeners and doers of the Word of God.

Prayer:
1. I receive grace to listen and do the command of God Almighty, in Jesus' name.
2. I'll obey Your Word, O Lord God, in Jesus' name.

Day 340

It is written: "If anyone among you thinks he is religious, and does not bridle his tongue but deceives his own heart, this one's religion is useless. Pure and undefiled religion before God and the Father is this: to visit orphans and widows in their trouble, and to keep oneself unspotted from the world" (James 1:26-27).

Principle: Never neglect caring for the orphans, widows, and the needy.

Prayer: 1. I repent of neglecting the care of the needy, O God; forgive me, in Jesus' name.

2. O Lord God, open my eyes to see the needs of people around me, in Jesus' name.

Day 341

It is written: "Have you not shown partiality among yourselves, and become judges with evil thoughts?" (James 2:4).

Principle: Never be guided by wrong motives or they will affect your actions.

Prayer: 1. I repent of my wrong motives, O God; forgive me, in Jesus' name.

2. O Lord God, guide me by Your Holy Spirit against discrimination, in Jesus' name.

Day 342

It is written: "What does it profit, my brethren, if someone says he has faith but does not have works? Can faith save him? Thus also faith by itself, if it does not have works, is dead. But do you want to know, O foolish man, that faith without works is dead?" (James 2:14, 17, 20).

Principle: Your struggle against fear becomes ineffective and worthless if it lacks faith and action.

Prayer:
1. I receive grace to add good works to my faith, in Jesus' name.
2. I shall not be ineffective in overcoming fear, in Jesus' name.

DAY 343

It is written: "Even so the tongue is a little member and boasts great things. See how great a forest a little fire kindles! And the tongue is a fire, a world of iniquity. The tongue is so set among our members that it defiles the whole body, and sets on fire the course of nature; and it is set on fire by hell. But no man can tame the tongue. It is an unruly evil, full of deadly poison. With it we bless our God and Father, and with it we curse men, who have been made in the similitude of God. Out of the same mouth proceed blessing and cursing. My brethren, these things ought not to be so" (James 3:5-6, 8-10).

Principle: To conquer fear, tame your tongue. It could ruin you or bless you.

Prayer:
1. I subject my tongue to the controlling power of the Holy Spirit, in Jesus' name.
2. My tongue shall not ruin me, but bless me, in Jesus' name.

Day 344

It is written: "For where envy and self-seeking exist, confusion and every evil thing are there" (James 3:16).

Principle: Victory over fear should not be just for selfish ambition, but to set your life right.

Prayer:
1. I break free from every rivalry, disharmony, and rebellion, in Jesus' name.
2. I receive rest from confusion, in Jesus' name.

Day 345

It is written: "But the wisdom that is from above is first pure, then peaceable, gentle, willing to yield, full of mercy and good fruits, without partiality and without hypocrisy" (James 3:17).

Principle: Are you peace-loving, yet fearful? Compassionate, yet afraid? Wholeheartedly hold on, and be free from doubts, wavering, and insincerity.

Prayer: 1. I wholeheartedly hold on to God Almighty, for wisdom against fear, in Jesus' name.

2. In the name of Jesus, I'm free from doubts, wavering, and insincerity.

Day 346

It is written: "Now the fruit of righteousness is sown in peace by those who make peace" (James 3:18).

Principle: "And those who are peacemakers will plant seeds of peace and reap a harvest of goodness" (NLT).

Prayer:
1. I receive a peaceful mind, free from fears, agitating passions, and moral conflicts, in Jesus' name.
2. I sow in peace to all mankind and reap goodness, in Jesus' name.

Day 347

It is written: "Therefore submit to God. Resist the devil and he will flee from you" (James 4:7).

Principle: Subjecting yourself to God Almighty makes you stand firm against fear.

Prayer:
1. I humble myself before God to defeat my fears, in Jesus' name.
2. I take a firm stand against fear and worrying to walk in perpetual victory, in Jesus' name.

DAY 348

It is written: "Do not speak evil of one another, brethren. He who speaks evil of a brother and judges his brother, speaks evil of the law and judges the law. But if you judge the law, you are not a doer of the law but a judge. There is one Lawgiver, who is able to save and to destroy. Who are you to judge another?" (James 4:11-12).

Principle: When you condemn others, you give them the right to condemn you.

Prayer:
1. I repent of condemning others, O God; please forgive me, in Jesus' name.
2. I break free from the yoke of condemnation, in Jesus' name.

Day 349

It is written: "For whatever is born of God overcomes the world. And this is the victory that has overcome the world—our faith. Who is he who overcomes the world, but he who believes that Jesus is the Son of God?" (1 John 5:4-5).

Principle: "For every child of God defeats this evil world by trusting Christ to give the victory … " (NLT).

Prayer:
1. I believe that Jesus Christ is the Son of God, Who loves me and gave Himself for me.
2. I overcome my fears through the suffering, death, and resurrection of my Lord and Savior, Jesus Christ.

Victory Over Fear of Death

"Shall I yield to the whisper of fear, and give up the battle, and with it give up all hope? Far from it."
—Charles H. Spurgeon

Day 350

It is written: "But God will redeem my soul from the power of the grave, For He shall receive me" (Ps. 49:15).

Principle: God is all powerful, who is able to redeem you from the fear of death—trust Him.

Prayer: 1. Jesus paid the price to buy me out of the fear of death, so I'm free, in Jesus' name.

2. Thank You, my Lord Jesus Christ, for redeeming my life from death, hell, and the grave, in Jesus' name.

Day 351

It is written: "Let the groaning of the prisoner come before You; according to the greatness of Your power preserve those who are appointed to die" (Ps.79:11).

Principle: Fear of death condemns you to death, but fear of God brings you to life.

Prayer:
1. O Lord God, demonstrate Your power in my life as You break me free from attacks of death, hell, and the grave, in Jesus' name.
2. Through the blood of Jesus, I refute every condemnation of death over my life, in Jesus' name.

DAY 352

It is written: "With long life I will satisfy him, and show him My salvation" (Ps. 91:16).

Principle: Only God Almighty, the Giver of life, satisfies with long life and condemns fear of death—call upon Him and He will answer you.

Prayer: 1. O Lord God Almighty, satisfy me with long life and prosperity, in Jesus' name.

2. Attack of death on my life, be condemned, in Jesus' name.

Day 353

It is written: "I said, 'O my God, do not take me away in the midst of my days; Your years are throughout all generations'" (Ps. 102:24).

Principle: The eternal power of God can terminate your fear of death and give you length of days.

Prayer:
1. Eternal power of God, break me free from the attack of death and hell, in Jesus' name.
2. Thank You, Almighty God, for making me to fulfill my days with long life and peace, in Jesus' name.

Day 354

It is written: "For You have delivered my soul from death, my eyes from tears, and my feet from falling" (Ps. 116:8).

Principle: Fear of death fills eyes with tears and makes feet to stumble, but you can escape the traps.

Prayer: 1. Thank You, God Almighty, for You have delivered my soul from death, in Jesus' name.

2. My feet are kept from stumbling, in Jesus' name.

Day 355

It is written: "I shall not die, but live, and declare the works of the LORD" (Ps. 118:17).

Principle: You're alive as a living proof of God's wonderful power to testify of His goodness.

Prayer:
1. I proclaim of God's wonderful works in my life with thanksgiving, in Jesus' name.
2. I decree to my life, "I shall not die, but live and declare the works of the Lord," in Jesus' name.

Day 356

It is written: "The sting of death is sin, and the strength of sin is the law. But thanks be to God, who gives us the victory through our Lord Jesus Christ" (1 Cor. 15:55-57).

Principle: Fear of death is a sting to your soul—flush it out.

Prayer: 1. Blood of Jesus, flush the sting of death out of my life, in Jesus' name.

2. Attacks of death and its venom on my life shall not prosper, in Jesus' name.

Day 357

It is written: "Who delivered us from so great a death, and does deliver us; in whom we trust that He will still deliver us" (2 Cor. 1:10).

Principle: Confidence in God Almighty gives continuous victory over death.

Prayer:
1. I claim continuous victory over fear of death, in Jesus' name.
2. The pursuit of death and hell over my life is annulled by the blood of Jesus, in Jesus' name.

Day 358

It is written: "Then Death and Hades were cast into the lake of fire. This is the second death" (Rev. 20:14).

Principle: Death, too, has an end—the lake of fire—so death is not your end.

Prayer: 1. The power of the lake of fire shall have no hold over my life, in Jesus' name.

2. Through the blood of Jesus, I escape the torture of death and hell, in Jesus' name.

VICTORY OVER FEAR OF SICKNESS AND DISEASE

"The Lord has sustained us, and kept us above all real fear of evil, even when our spirit has been overwhelmed."

—Charles H. Spurgeon

Day 359

It is written: "And the LORD will take away from you all sickness, and will afflict you with none of the terrible diseases of Egypt which you have known, but will lay them on all those who hate you" (Deut. 7:15).

Principle: Fear of sickness and disease can be terror to your soul, but God can protect you from them.

Prayer:
1. I repent of my fear of sickness and disease, O God; forgive me, in Jesus' name.
2. In Your mercies, O God, heal me and cure all my diseases, in Jesus' name.

DAY 360

It is written: "The Spirit of God has made me, and the breath of the Almighty gives me life" (Job 33:4).

Principle: God Almighty owns your breath and your spirit; you need not fear.

Prayer:
1. My breath and my spirit are dedicated to Jesus Christ and to the power of His blood, in Jesus' name.
2. My breath and my spirit are preserved by God Almighty, in Jesus' name.

Day 361

It is written: "Many are the afflictions of the righteous, but the LORD delivers him out of them all. He guards all his bones; not one of them is broken" (Ps. 34:19-20).

Principle: You may face many troubles, yet God's protection is certain; trust Him.

Prayer: 1. Thank You, God Almighty, for rescuing me from afflictions, in Jesus' name.

2. Thank You, God Almighty, for keeping my soul from destruction, in Jesus' name.

Day 362

It is written: "Surely He has borne our griefs and carried our sorrows; yet we esteemed Him stricken, smitten by God, and afflicted. But He was wounded for our transgressions, He was bruised for our iniquities; the chastisement for our peace was upon Him, And by His stripes we are healed" (Isa. 53:4-5).

Principle: Weaknesses and sorrows of heart could crush your soul, but Jesus bore them all.

Prayer:
1. Thank You, my Lord Jesus Christ, for bearing my grief and sorrows, in Jesus' name.
2. I have peace through the sufferings and punishments of my Lord Jesus Christ, in Jesus' name.

Day 363

It is written: "Heal me, O LORD, and I shall be healed; save me, and I shall be saved, for You are my praise" (Jer. 17:14).

Principle: Sicknesses and diseases could make you cry, but a cry unto God Almighty cures the incurable.

Prayer:
1. I praise God Almighty, because He is most powerful and mighty to heal me, in Jesus' name.
2. I am saved from sickness unto life, in Jesus' name.

Day 364

It is written: "Bless the LORD, O my soul; and all that is within me, bless His holy name! Bless the LORD, O my soul, and forget not all His benefits: Who forgives all your iniquities, who heals all your diseases, who redeems your life from destruction, who crowns you with lovingkindness and tender mercies, who satisfies your mouth with good things, so that your youth is renewed like the eagle's" (Ps. 103:1-5).

Principle: "Forget not all His benefits … ." Benefits such as: forgiveness of sins, healing all diseases, ransom from death, and surrounding you with love and tender mercies.

Prayer:
1. I celebrate the benefits of God Almighty in my life with thanksgiving, in Jesus' name.
2. Divine benefits shall never cease in my life, in Jesus' name.

DAY 365

It is written: "He sent His word and healed them, and delivered them from their destructions" (Ps. 107:20).

Principle: God's Word is powerful to the rescuing from the pit of hell and death.

Prayer: 1. Thank You, Almighty God, for rescuing me from the pit of hell and death, in Jesus' name.

2. As the Lord God Almighty lives and His Spirit lives. The power of fear is defeated in my life, in Jesus' name.

Contact the Author at:

www.davidkomolafe.authorweblog.com

Visit the author's website at

www.davidkomolafe.com

To order additional copies of this book,
please visit www.redemption-press.com.

Printed in the USA
CPSIA information can be obtained
at www.ICGtesting.com
CBHW061105240724
12037CB00025B/751